Science for Every Learner

Brain-Compatible Pathways to Scientific Literacy

Kathleen Carroll

Zephyr Press

Tucson, Arizona

About Zephyr Press

Founded in 1979 in Tucson, Arizona, Zephyr Press continually strives to provide quality, innovative products for our customers, with the goal of improving learning opportunities for all children. With a focus on gifted education, multiple intelligences, and brain-compatible learning, Zephyr Press material is selected to help *all* children reach their highest potential.

Science for Every Learner
Brain-Compatible Pathways to Scientific Literacy

Grades: K–12

© 2000 by Kathleen Carroll
Printed in the United States of America

ISBN 1-56976-105-1

Editors: Veronica Durie and Stacey Shropshire
Cover design: Daniel Miedaner
Design and production: Daniel Miedaner
Illustrations: Steve Carroll and Sandy Perkins

Published by:
Zephyr Press
P.O. Box 66006
Tucson, AZ 85728-6006
1-800-232-2187
www.zephyrpress.com
www.i-home-school.com

 Zephyr Press is a registered trademark of Zephyr Press, Inc.

Library of Congress Cataloging-in-Publication Data

Carroll, Kathleen, 1946–
    Science for every learner : brain-compatible pathways to scientific literacy / Kathleen Carroll.
        p. cm.
    Includes bibliographical references.
    ISBN 1-56976-105-1 (alk. paper)
    1. Science—Study and teaching (Elementary)—Activity programs—United States. 2. Cognitive styles—United States. I. Title.

LB1585.3 .C37 2000
372.3'5—dc21   99-057922

Contents

Acknowledgments

Many people have contributed to the production of this book and CD. Steve Carroll, my husband, illustrator, and savior in computer crises, has been a constant source of inspiration and support. My good friend Robert Cohen, creator of the taxonomy used throughout the discovery phases, spent many hours in conversations with me about how to change "cookbook science" activities into real inquiry projects. Veronica Durie, my editor, has kept me going with her enthusiasm and wise guidance. John Grassi of Cambridge College was my first inspiration for making songs and stories about science topics.

Contributors to studies include science teachers Margaret Jackson and Theresa Hill; monarch butterfly experts Jewell Stoddart, formerly of the Cheshire Cat Bookstore; Karen Oberhauser of the University of Minnesota; Chip Taylor at the University of Kansas and current head of Monarch Watch; Dan Hillburn of the Department of Agriculture in Oregon; Paul Runquist of Monarch Magic in Oregon; Neil Davidson of the University of Maryland; and Jim Brady, consultant. Mardy Burgess wrote the cell description in the story for the Living Things Study. Thanks to Barbara Bourbon for contributing the idea and the term "accidental science."

Special thanks to physics teacher Paul O'Herron, ecologist Bernie Nebel, classical music composer Nicholas Maw, and electric expert William Beaty for helping to hunt out misconceptions. Any that may still remain are my own responsibility.

Thanks, too, to the twenty-two singers, musicians, and actors listed on page 155 who contributed their energy and talent to the audiotape that can be purchased to accompany this book. Special appreciation goes to Gwen Jenifer, the musical director; Joe Brady, singer, songwriter, and musician; and Ruth Turner, singer, musician, and outstanding helper.

Introduction

The goal of this book and CD is to provide the teacher with a motivating and effective format for all kinds of students to enjoy learning science processes and content, and to develop scientific habits of mind. Scientists often report that their passion for the field arose from exciting experiences with science during childhood. People who don't like science, however, often perceive it as a heartless, lifeless subject based on dry facts and theories. Much of the focus of *Science for Every Learner* is on helping students develop a heartfelt connection to science without sacrificing mental rigor. I hope this connection will help students develop a lifelong interest in the subject.

Format

The *Science for Every Learner (SEL)* Format for Understanding, is a blueprint for teachers to use to design effective learning experiences for a variety of learners. The format has suggestions for preparation where the teacher formulates the "big question" or essence of the study, uses a domain matrix to check alignment between planned activities and objectives, then prepares the room and finds out what students already know (Getting Ready). Once the preparations are in place, the main aspects of the format structure the study:

Discovering the Concepts: Students immerse themselves in the subject matter through hands-on data collection and organization followed by sharing and processing.

Creating the Context: Students begin to see where their discoveries fit into the big picture of the study through stories and plays. Some of these are on the CD.

Deepening the Learning: Students make new emotional and intellectual connections to the subject matter of the study through multiple intelligences activities, including art and song. You will find songs about each of the studies on the CD.

Assessing the Understanding: Included are suggestions for journal and portfolio entries and Think Trix questions for formative assessment along the way. The study culminates with a performance task with a rubric to provide summative assessment.

In the Format for Understanding, students first make their own discoveries (Discovering the Concepts), then fit the discoveries into a bigger picture of the knowledge that already exists in the scientific realm (Creating the Context). They extend the new understandings through a variety of experiences and reflections (Deepening the Learning), and finally demonstrate their ability to transfer by applying the understanding to new situations (Assessing the Understanding). This format is compatible with recent brain research that indicates the importance of taking in data to construct knowledge, the value of understanding the big picture to see where the knowledge fits in the broader scheme, and the necessity of emotional connections for motivation and retention, including engaging students in real-world challenges. Specific elements of brain research in relation to the format are discussed in the pages that follow.

The Format for Understanding is geared to help students attain the levels of science literacy called for in the National Science Education Standards. The basic principles listed in the National Science Education Standards are that all students can learn science and should have the opportunity to become scientifically literate. According to the National Science Education Standards a person who is scientifically literate can do the following:

- ▶ ask, find, or determine answers to questions that arise from curiosity about everyday experiences
- ▶ describe, explain, and predict natural phenomena
- ▶ read and understand articles about science and have social conversations about the validity of the conclusions
- ▶ identify scientific issues that underlie local and national issues, and express informed positions
- ▶ evaluate the quality of scientific information based on its source and the methods used to generate it

The standards suggest that scientific literacy grows and deepens over a lifetime. The attitudes and values that form its foundation, however, are established in the early years. A correlation between the standards and the format is also provided in the following pages.

There are three main underpinnings of the Format for Understanding, all of which are in keeping with the latest brain research and the National Science Standards: constructivism, Accelerated Learning, and the movement toward more authentic assessments.

First, we need to consider constructivism in relation to a more traditional approach to learning. In a traditional approach, students passively take in information, then practice and repeat that information to embed it in memory. But psychological research indicates that there are more effective ways for learning to take place (Resnick 1987). Learners often approach a new learning task with prior knowledge and beliefs. By interacting with the subject matter, they construct their own meanings.

Constructivism is based on the premise that deep learning occurs when students' former beliefs about a subject no longer prove to be sufficient. Through active exploration, students construct new understandings that are more in keeping with the evidence than their old beliefs. Fosmet (1993) notes that Brooks and Brooks have outlined five overarching principles for constructivism: "1. posing problems of emerging relevance to learners; 2. structuring learning around 'big ideas' or primary concepts; 3. seeking and valuing students' points of view; 4. adapting curriculum to address students' suppositions; and 5. assessing student learning in the context of teaching" (viii). In science, active exploration usually involves working with materials in activities that motivate students intrinsically. In the discovery phase (page xiv), for example, the format uses Cohen's taxonomy, which provides a step-by-step process that encourages students to construct their meaning.

Second, let us look at how Accelerated Learning contributes to the Format for Understanding. A constructivist approach to learning needs to be balanced with the assurance that students can test their constructed learning against essential knowledge that has developed over time in a particular domain. Accelerated Learning provides this balance.

Accelerated Learning draws on the research of Georgi Lozanov, a Bulgarian psychiatrist and educator who spent many years investigating the optimal conditions to enhance human learning. An Accelerated Learning classroom presents students with the big picture, an overview of what they are going to learn, so that they can see how the various pieces fit. Then it uses stories, games, laughter, and music, all of which artfully lead students to take in large amounts of information effortlessly. Peripheral elements, such as posters, artwork, and key vocabulary words, decorate the walls so that the *paraconscious,* the part of the mind that is conscious but not focused, absorbs new words and images without noticing. Accelerated Learning techniques allow students to experience material visually, auditorally, and physically, which accommodates a wide range of learning styles and creates more dendritic connections in the brain. The artistic endeavors also help them develop emotional connections to the subject matter; that is, to care more deeply about learning it. Lozanov's research, along with the work of other educators who built on his findings, is designed to use a balance of linear and holistic methods to make education more natural and joyful.

Finally, we can see how authentic assessment is integral to the Format for Understanding. Authentic, ongoing assessments guarantee meaningful evaluation of students' developing understanding throughout the learning process. According to Wiggins and McTighe (1998), "Greater coherence among desired results, key performances, and teaching and learning experiences leads to better student performance—the purpose of design" (9). The assessments in the format are all geared to create a cohesiveness among the objectives, the assessments, and the teaching and learning experiences. The products to assess include portfolios and journals (page xii). Frank Lyman's Think Trix, a graphic method for including higher-level thinking skills, is included early on to give examples of questions you can ask throughout the unit to ensure students understand at deep levels (page xii). Performance tasks give students opportunities to transfer their learning to new situations, an indication of true understanding (page xiv). The format also provides a domain matrix (page viii), a powerful tool to assess the alignment between the outcomes and objectives, and the activities and assessments.

Following is a discussion of each element you will find in the units.

Big Questions

In *MindShifts*, Caine, Caine, and Crowell describe the search for meaning as innate. The big questions provide a focus; the answers to the questions will be the "meaning" for which students search. Big questions focus on what matters most. The big questions reflect the essence of a particular study. Grant Wiggins and Jay McTighe (1998) outline some criteria for determining that essence:

- A study must have enduring value beyond the classroom. The essence of what students learn from the study is an understanding worth an adult's knowing.
- The ideas reside at the heart of the discipline, involving students in the activities in which professionals within the discipline engage.
- The study must uncover misconceptions.
- The study must have the potential to engage students, connecting to their interests.

Big questions keep a study focused on what is most important.

Domain Matrix

The domain matrix is a powerful, easy-to-use tool. The outcomes, objectives, activities, and assessments come directly from the big question.

Goals
- To help the teacher align outcomes and objectives with activities and assessments
- To assess the validity of particular activities and assessments; to answer the question, "Do these activities actually teach and assess the listed objectives?"
- To determine whether each objective is adequately addressed

Brain Connections
The search for meaning is innate in humans. The domain matrix enables teachers to stay true to what is most important and meaningful in a study.

National Science Education Standards
The standards note the importance of planning. Their purpose is to present the district, state, and national goals in ways that align with the interests and experiences available to students. Teachers design activities and assessments that facilitate deep understanding. Assessment standard C, for example, requires that the feature that a teacher claims to measure is actually measured. The domain matrix is an ideal tool to help teachers ensure this standard is met.

Designing Your Own Domain Matrix
You can create your own domain matrix when you develop other units of study, either as extensions of this book or others. Following is a procedure for creating a domain matrix:

1. List the outcomes and objectives you hope to achieve with the study, based on the big question and ongoing goals you have for your class.

2. Briefly describe the activities for the study.
3. Put key words from the outcomes and objectives across the top of the matrix. If necessary, you can use letters to represent the outcomes, with an explanation below that links the letters with the outcomes.
4. Put key words representing the activities for the study down the left side of the matrix. If necessary, you can use numbers for the activities, with an explanation nearby linking the letters with the outcomes.
5. Place check marks or Xs in the cells to indicate the specific activities that accomplish specific outcomes.
6. To assess your plan, note which activities support the most outcomes. Note the activities that support only one or a few outcomes. Notice if there are some outcomes that lack activities.

Activities and Assessments	Outcomes and Objectives				
	Research	Scientific Inquiry	Problem Solving	Teamwork	Appropriate Units
Discovering	X	X	X	X	X
Plays and Stories				X	X
MI Activities	X	X	X	X	X
Think Trix				X	X
Journal	X	X	X	X	X
Portfolio	X	X	X	X	X
Performance Task	X	X	X	X	X

Getting Ready

Place some posters or banners around the room that introduce and reinforce vocabulary and concepts a few days before the study begins. As the study proceeds, it will benefit students if they make some of these peripherals, because the design and production contribute to student learning. Before beginning a unit, students make Mind Maps summarizing their knowledge of the topic. At the end of the unit, they make more Mind Maps showing their new understandings.

Goals

- To enable students to learn vocabulary easily through the use of peripherals
- To enable students to see the growth of their knowledge over time through the use of Mind Maps

Brain Connections

Eric Jensen (1998) points out that more than 90 percent of the information that comes into the brain is visual. Colorful visual aids, or peripherals, that change often get and keep the brain's attention. A study by Lozanov (1981) shows that peripherals increased learning over time. Caine, Caine, and Crowell (1999) state that the brain absorbs information that lies beyond the field of direct vision. This is the information that one perceives out of the "side of the eye," so to speak. Peripheral information can be purposely organized to facilitate learning.

Jensen (1994) describes Edelman's view that memory is changing all the time, taking in new information and revising old beliefs. The conscious reordering of learning through Mind Mapping is a way to keep the learning dynamic and put it into long-term memory.

National Science Education Standards

The standards define scientific literacy as the appropriate use of scientific terms, concepts, and processes. Helping students learn the terms through peripherals is one aspect of scientific literacy.

Teaching Students How to Mind Map

A Mind Map provides an immediate, whole-brain way to help students organize what they know. A Mind Map reflects the way the brain stores information—like branches on a tree.

- Start with a title and picture of your topic in the center of your paper. Branch out from the central idea with key words and pictures, one to a line. Research shows that key words are easier to read than sentences, and that pictures enhance memory and creativity.

- Use arrows to connect ideas.

- Use various sizes of letters, boxes, stars, exclamation points, and asterisks to show emphasis.

- Use color to aid memory, emphasize important points, and organize the information.

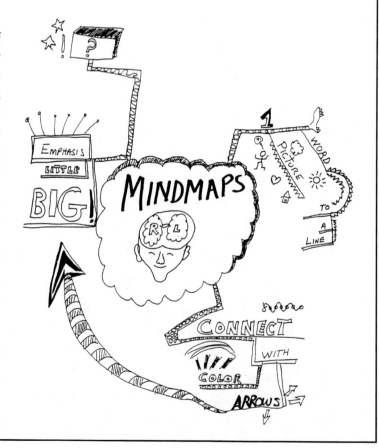

Assessing Understanding

Any assessment must grow out of the big questions, the objectives, and the desired outcomes for an activity. That is, the assessment tool should accurately evaluate whether the student's performance in an activity met the objective of the activity.

Goals

- To support students in learning the content and processes
- To apprise students of their current strengths and next steps needed to expand their knowledge or skill in a particular subject
- To help students acquire self-assessment skills and develop personal responsibility for their learning as they question and reflect on their work
- To help you evaluate your own practice
- To grade students' performance

Brain Connections

Research shows that real-world projects, as called for in the science standards, tap into students' best abilities and motivation. Marion Diamond's research (D'Arcangelo 1998) indicates that the most enriched environment is the real world. We may also be able to enhance brain growth by giving students real-world challenges, such as public performances, or performance tasks.

National Science Education Standards

The standards state, "When students are engaged in assessment tasks that are similar in form to tasks in which they will engage in their lives outside the classroom or that are similar to the activities of scientists, great confidence can be attached to the data collected" (83). That is, the standards recommend that students be involved in authentic assessment tasks, tasks that the adults in the profession are likely to engage in. The standards recommend emphasizing assessment of what is highly valued rather than what is easy to measure, a project rather than a paper-and-pencil test. The standards also recommend assessing scientific understanding rather than an accumulation of scientific facts, and assessing students based on what they can prove they know rather than looking for what they don't know. Finally, the standards recommend that you assess along the way and allow students to assess their own work and that of their peers rather than doing one end-of-term assessment.

As students develop self-assessment tools, they develop personal responsibility for their learning as they question and reflect on their own work. You can also use the tools to evaluate your own practice. Last and least, assessment tools are a way to determine grades.

The assessment tools used in the studies in this book are ongoing. That is, you will assess students' progress and understanding, guiding them to evaluate their own work as they go instead of basing it solely on a final product at the end of the unit. The assessment tools are also authentic, performance based, and valuable within the scientific community. Following are the assessment tools used in this book.

Think Trix

Think Trix is a questioning method, formulated by retired University of Maryland Professor Frank Lyman, that has been used successfully in many Maryland classrooms. Often, in classrooms, questioning requires only basic-knowledge responses. Think Trix questions encourage thinking to extend beyond this level.

The simple graphic anchors provided opposite will help you and your students regularly address a variety of thinking skills. The questioning examples given serve as models to help students to develop their own higher-level questions.

Good, open-ended questions motivate children to think more deeply and expand their ability to solve problems. As students answer these sorts of questions, you can learn more about how individual students think. Good questions provide ongoing assessment of student understanding. Students' responses to these questions will reveal how deeply they understand the content and skills they are learning.

Developing Think Trix Questions

Just about any question can fit into a Think Trix category. Some questions could fit into more than one, depending on the response you are looking for. For practice, you might categorize the questions mentioned in the discovery phase of this introduction. The Think Trix graphics, or icons, can remind you to go beyond the simple recall questions that dominate many classrooms. You might consider each category of question as an opportunity to exercise a different "muscle" in your students' and your own minds. Some muscles may be strong; some may have atrophied. Examples of Think Trix questions are provided in each unit. Use the examples to develop your own questions.

You can also display the icons on the wall or CD them to each student's desk to remind them to ask questions at all of the levels. As students become familiar with the various patterns of thinking represented by the icons, they become more discerning about answering questions and solving problems. They can simply ask themselves, "What kind of thinking is this question or problem asking for?" Opposite are the icons for Think Trix along with word prompts to assist in developing questions for each icon.

Journals and Portfolios

Students will use journals in a variety of ways:

- To record and organize observations
- To reflect on their learning and on themselves as learners
- To assess their learning of the content and processes
- To compile questions, plan how to answer the questions, and record the research that leads them to those answers

Portfolios promote a climate of reflection in the classroom. They give students the sense of their own history as learners and allow them to reflect and process their learning.

The portfolios students will compile for the studies in this book can include written works, artwork, photographs, CDs and videoCDs of presentations, as well as

Think Trix Icons

Recall
define, design, list, detail, summarize

Cause<>Effect
postulate, note, consider motive, infer, predict, hypothesize

Difference
contrast, compare, distinguish, differentiate, discern

Similarity
make analogy, compare, examine

Ideas to Example(s)
categorize, deduce, substantiate, make analogy, support

Example(s) to Idea(s)
classify, induce, conclude, generalize, find essence

Evaluation
consider ethics, evaluate, judge, rate, weigh evidence

scientific investigations, products from extension activities, excerpts from journals, documentation of a process a student followed to finish a product, and reflections on selected work.

You need to decide how you will assess the portfolio. Will you set up criteria and standards ahead of time? Will students help you determine the criteria and standards? Will the focus be on overall excellence, or on growth over time? Will you develop rubrics to help guide students as they go?

Brain Connections

According to Caine, Caine, and Crowell (1999), a great deal of the effort put into teaching and studying is wasted because students do not adequately process their experiences. In *The Brains behind the Brain,* D'Arcangelo (1998) interviewed five brain experts. Eric Jensen is quoted as stating that downtime or processing time is something students must have and therefore will take, whether we give them the opportunity or not. Journals and portfolios are natural vehicles for such processing and reflecting. In journals, students reflect on and process as they develop their work, and you can track their progress by reading what they have written.

Performance Tasks

Performance tasks are products or performances. They require an ability to apply facts, concepts, or skills. Often students can contribute to the design of motivating and meaningful performance tasks and rubrics. See opposite and page xv.

Brain Connections

Performance tasks involve the emotional parts of the brain. Making a product or engaging in a performance requires an emotional investment because it reflects the creators or performer's personality. Public demonstrations are particularly useful because, as Eric Jensen (1995) points out, students experience "anticipation, concern, excitement, and suspense."

The process for creating strong performance tasks is adapted from *A Teacher's Guide to Performance-Based Learning and Assessment* by K. Michael Hibbard and the teachers of Connecticut's Pompraug School District 15. Some of the suggestions are from Jay McTighe's *Eight-Step Process for Designing Performance Assessments* and the *Educational Leadership* article "What Happens between Assessments?"

Discovering the Concepts

The purpose of the discovery phase is for students to discover information themselves (the constructivist approach). The phase is designed to support students in constructing their own sense of the concepts to be presented. The discovery phase is organized around the first four stages of Robert Cohen's Taxonomy for Discovery: *experiencing, organizing, sharing,* and *processing.*

Robert Cohen did his undergraduate work in mathematics at the University of Chicago and went on to teach college mathematics. He was asked to teach a course to elementary education majors. He gave students in that class the Kolb Learning Styles Inventory and found out that they tested as concrete, active learners. By contrast,

Process for Creating Performance Tasks

Background

The work students have done up to this point should have prepared them to transfer knowledge to a new situation.

Task

Explain your instructional objectives to students and ask them to design a performance or product that meets those objectives. The task should be meaningful to students, relating to real-world issues and problems. Grant Wiggins suggests brainstorming responses to the stem "The students understand the idea only when they can . . ." will help you design the most effective tasks. Understanding in this context means the ability to apply the essential knowledge, the content and processes learned, to new situations.

Audience

Name a real or imaginary audience for students' product or performance. Research shows that real audiences motivate and excite students.

Purpose

Show the students why this is a worthwhile project in terms of the goals of this course or subject. The project could also be worthwhile because it provides a service to members of the community.

Procedure

Outline the steps the students must take to complete the task, in sequence. Determine which steps will be assessed.

Assessment

Design a rubric that provides the criteria and standards by which the task will be assessed. Give the students the rubric so they have it while they are working on the task so they know what they are working toward. The rubrics used in this book (an example is on page 24) are particularly well suited to student and parent use. Notice that the indicators down the left-hand column provide a holistic picture of excellence in the performance. The rubric also provides for analytical assessment as the work is developing and at the completion of the performance. For each criterion, students can see where they are and what it takes to reach the next level.

Steps for Developing Effective Performance Rubrics

1. Determine criteria that come directly from the performance task, represent the elements necessary for true understanding of the big question, reflect the most valued elements of student performance, and reflect the outcomes and objectives listed in the domain matrix.
2. Write the criteria down the left side of the rubric chart.
3. Develop standards that clearly delineate different levels of quality. Avoid the temptation to include words such as "most," "some," or "few" in the standards. Looking at student work can help you write indicators that give a true picture of excellent, average, and below-average work.
4. Write the levels across the top of the chart to represent *advanced, intermediate, beginning.* Make the levels appropriate and interesting as on page 120.
5. If you need to determine a letter grade, multiply the levels by the number of criteria. For example, if your rubric has three levels and four criteria, a perfect score would be twelve. Next, determine a numerical score for each level based on the number of levels you have. For example, in a rubric with three levels, an *advanced* indicator might be worth three points, *intermediate* would be worth two, and *beginning* would be worth one. Calculate the percentage of the total possible to determine the letter grade.
6. Plan to revise. Student feedback is an important step in the revision process.

Steps for Developing Effective Performance Rubrics with Students

When students have an opportunity to help create rubrics, they develop the ability to discern quality, an important ability for a life-long learner. Following are steps in the process that students may help with:

1. Establish criteria. Show students good and poor examples or benchmarks from another class, or that you have designed. Lead them to determine the criteria that make the examples good or poor. Give them practice assessing themselves and peers using the criteria; don't add the standards.
2. Develop standards. Reexamine the good and poor benchmarks you used before or show new ones. Brainstorm excellent, acceptable, and unacceptable levels for each criterion. Write the criteria down the left and the levels across the top of a chart paper. Put students in groups and ask each group to address one criterion. Ask each group to develop indicators for each level of the criterion they are addressing. Ask the whole class to critique the indicators. You can ask them these questions: Does the indicator give you a clear picture of what a learner at this level does? Are the words used precise and concrete, words that everyone will agree upon (for example, *creativity* is an abstract, subjective word that may not be effective as an indicator)? Are the different levels clearly differentiated?
3. Use the rubric. Make one copy of the completed rubric for each student. Ask students to self- or peer-assess while you assess, too. Compare the results and discuss misunderstandings.
4. Revise the rubric as necessary.

math professors tested as abstract, reflective learners. Cohen realized he needed to teach according to the students' learning styles rather than his own. Constructivist theory also suggests that learners move from the concrete and active to the abstract and reflective. Cohen developed a taxonomy for discovery learning that moved students from the concrete toward the abstract. The taxonomy maintains a sense of scientific rigor that involves and excites students. It requires learners to engage in the same processes that scientists and mathematicians do. As I have used the taxonomy, I have seen that students systematically improved their skills in observing and collecting data, finding patterns, communicating, and processing. As a result, they are often able to develop strong hypotheses worth testing.

To lay the foundations for the ability to transfer learning, give students the following learning opportunities:

- Concrete experiences that require the use of their senses to observe what happens (experiencing)
- Finding patterns and organizing data based on those patterns (organizing)
- Verbalizing thinking with others to clarify understandings and make tentative generalizations about principles (sharing)
- Reflecting on the subject, gradually becoming aware of previous misconceptions, thoughtfully constructing meaning from the new experiences, and integrating new understandings with previous knowledge (processing)

Brain Connections

Experiencing

Lawrence Lowery (1997) points out that the brain must take in data to construct knowledge. That data comes in through the senses. Hands-on experiences pique students' interest and link the perceptions stored within the brain; nonverbal data enrich the verbal.

Organizing

Eric Jensen (1998) points out that pattern making is essential for the brain to make meaning. Learners need data from which to extract patterns (95). For learners who lack a wide range of knowledge, hands-on experiential learning provides the data necessary for the patterns to develop and for deep meaning to emerge. Caine (D'Arcangelo 1998) notes that "Every human being is driven to reach for meaning. We all try to create patterns from our environment" (23).

Sharing

Caine (D'Arcangelo 1998) says that we all learn to some extent through interaction with others (24). Because ours is a social brain, comparing our own perceptions with those of others is a necessary step in learning.

Processing

According to Jensen and Caine (D'Arcangelo 1998), the brain needs time to reflect on learning (25). Processing enables the brain to create personal meaning, which is necessary for long-term memory to take place.

National Science Education Standards

The standards advocate a change in emphasis in science teaching. They call for a greater emphasis on student understanding than on mere acquisition of knowledge. This emphasis includes engaging students in active scientific inquiry processes and the analysis and organization of data. Another strong theme in the standards is that learning is an active process whereby enthusiastic and motivated students build or construct their own knowledge in a process that is individual and social. The standards state that reflection and processing are necessary for students to establish connections between their current knowledge and the new learning.

Using Cohen's Taxonomy for Discovery to Design Lessons

A constructivist approach put forward by the Taxonomy for Discovery suggests new roles for teachers and students. Rather than providing knowledge, teachers facilitate students in becoming observers, pattern finders, and theorizers. Cohen encourages teachers to create an atmosphere of fun and challenge as they dare students to take on each new role. Students need to be allowed to freely explore, observe, and collect data in their own ways.

With a little imagination, a teacher can turn cookbook, or step-by-step lessons, into constructivist lessons. Rather than telling students exactly what to do with the materials, give them some freedom to find out on their own. Sometimes a few guiding questions are all that is needed to direct students' attention toward the discovery at hand. Some of the following suggestions are drawn from Mary Lee Martin's article "Productive Questions: Tools for Supporting Constructivist Learning" (1999). Many suggestions come from conversations with Robert Cohen, designer of this taxonomy.

Stage 1	**Stage 2**	**Stage 3**	**Stage 4** (*This stage leads to a hypothesis*)
Experiencing	**Organizing**	**Sharing**	**Processing**
Doing (exploring)	Categorizing (tables, charts)	Comparing findings	Synthesizing findings
Observing (what happens)	Graphing	and ways of organizing	Writing in journals
Recording data	Pattern finding		

Experiencing

The students work individually or in small groups. They become involved in doing something right away. No theories allowed. Students use their senses to observe carefully and write down their observations.

To facilitate, encourage students to get into the doing first, then the observing, and finally the writing of their observations.

When they are doing, ask action-oriented questions, such as "What happens if . . . ?" "What would happen if . . . ?" "Can you find a way to . . . ?" "Can you figure out how to . . . ?"

When they are observing, ask attention-focusing questions as simple as "What do you observe?" If some students begin to get discouraged, you can ask, "What do you notice about . . . ? How does it look, feel, smell?" Ask measuring and counting questions to help students become more precise. "How many . . . ? How much . . . ? How long . . . ? How often . . . ?"

When they are writing, encourage students to write down every observation, listing anything that might be important. Let them know that there is no need to organize yet.

Organizing

Students look for patterns in the data they have collected and come up with a way to organize the data into groups. They may present the groupings in charts, tables, graphs, or other visual formats.

Facilitate by asking students to analyze and classify. "How are _____ similar or different? What goes together? How do they go together? What patterns do you see?"

Sharing

Students work together as a community of scientists. Students are fascinated to see the different things other people notice and compare ways they organize their findings. Students develop skills in speaking and listening. Students write comments and suggestions to the other individuals or groups.

Facilitate by encouraging students to articulate their findings clearly and listen well enough to restate others' findings and write helpful comments and suggestions. Ask students to notice differences in data. If there are disagreements, let students know that this is exactly what happens when professional scientists share their findings. Inform students of the value of disagreeing agreeably. Encourage students to observe together to resolve differences. Ask students to notice which organizations yield better results than others. This can support students in developing discernment.

Processing

Students integrate the data, synthesizing their findings through whole-group discussions followed by journal writing. Students begin to formulate hypotheses or theories they can test.

Facilitate by encouraging discussions, including reasoning and clarifying questions. "Why do you think . . . ? What is your reason for . . . ?" Challenge the thinking of other students. "Do you agree with . . . ? Why or why not?" Relate students' findings to currently agreed-upon scientific understandings. Help students verbalize their budding hypotheses: "What happens if . . . ?" "Can you invent a rule for . . . ?" Support students in beginning to formulate experimental procedures. "How could you prove that?" See page 1 for a unit on Science as Inquiry.

As students organize, share, and process the data, they begin to develop a theory or hypothesis. Cohen's taxonomy provides students with background experiences that naturally lead them to come up with logical hypotheses. Hypotheses emerge as they collect data and then look for patterns so they can organize it, share their findings with others, and process their findings with the group.

As hypotheses emerge, students can repeat the stages of the taxonomy. They gather their data at the experiencing stage, organize their findings, then share the results in small groups. Students process their learning with the whole class. A rubric for the Taxonomy for Discovery is available on page 148.

Creating a Context for the Discoveries: Plays and Stories

According to Bruner (1960), "teaching specific topics or skills without making clear their context in the broader fundamental structure of a field of knowledge is uneconomical. . . . An understanding of fundamental principles and ideas appears to be the main road to adequate transfer of training" (12).

Goals

- To give students opportunities to understand the big picture, or conceptual framework, regarding the subject
- To help students understand the discoveries they made as specific instances of more general circumstances
- To help students comprehend the current understandings among scientists about this subject so they can compare them with their own experiences and reflections, even if they did not reach the conclusions you expected
- To help students find the emotional hook by enhancing their personal association with the material through adventure, mystery, humor, or real-world relevance
- To help students develop their ability to make internal visual images that are useful for mathematical thinking and problem solving in general

Students perform the plays or actively read along as you play the CD. They can also create their own plays using the vocabulary and concepts of the study. The story can personify the concepts, describe an imaginary student who learns this new information, mimic a fairy tale, and so on. Sometimes making a Mind Map with the vocabulary and beginning concepts for a plot, followed by writing as quickly as possible without editing at first, can move the creative process along.

At the end of the unit, students can write their own plays or stories to demonstrate their new learning.

Students relax and effortlessly take in the information as you read the stories aloud or play the CD. Write a story that uses rich sensory descriptions and that asks the listener to be in the story. Incorporate the vocabulary and concepts of the study. Mind Mapping and writing quickly can work well here, too. As you read, play music with a slow beat (for example, concertos from the Baroque period by composers such as Bach and Vivaldi) softly in the background.

Prepare students for distractions, such as bells or announcements over the public address system. Make sure they are ready to resume the story if there is an interruption. Ask the students to sit back, relax, and picture in their minds the story they are about to hear. Immediately and frequently involve all the senses. Give students time to reorient themselves after the story. Ask students to write about or share their experiences. Many teachers have found this to be an effective way to elicit writing from formerly reluctant writers.

Brain Connections

Brain research emphasizes the importance of the big picture and the need for an emotional connection to learning. Marilee Sprenger (1999) points out that "emotional stimulus and novelty are the two biggest attention getters" (95). She also states that "emotional memory takes precedence over any other kind of memory" (54). Students' involvement in the plays and stories stimulates them emotionally in such a way.

National Science Education Standards

The Standards note a goal of students experiencing the richness and excitement of knowing about and understanding the natural world. Scientific literacy includes being able to appropriately use scientific terms, processes, and concepts. The plays and stories help students understand how the ideas they have been developing through inquiry fit into the larger scheme of things. They also help students develop the vocabulary and ability to speak about the concepts, processes, and phenomena they are studying.

Deepening the Learning through Multiple Intelligence Activities

Howard Gardner outlines his theory of multiple intelligences in *Frames of Mind* (1985). The theory suggests that there are six intelligences in addition to the logical-mathematical and verbal-linguistic that American schools and IQ tests focus on most heavily. They include visual-spatial, musical-rhythmic, bodily-kinesthetic, naturalist, interpersonal, and intrapersonal.

Each study contains suggestions for activities that reflect the intelligences, including making murals, flow charts, and illustrated books; role-playing, simulating situations, and doing projects; and learning songs and creating dances.

Goals

- To make more dendritic connections in the brain for deeper learning
- To create deeper emotional ties to the new learning
- To ask students to use their skills to apply the new knowledge to a variety of situations, and to make such transfers more likely
- To make more real-world connections

The suggestions on page xiii will help you get started in thinking of activities to do in your classroom. As you develop your own activities, allow students as much as possible, to choose activities they want to do while guiding them to try a variety of the activities.

Brain Connections

A multiple intelligence approach to learning connects with brain research in a number of ways. One criterion Howard Gardner uses to determine whether a skill constitutes an intelligence is if there is an area in the brain for that ability. In "Art for the Brain's Sake," Robert Sylwester (1998) points out that emotions drive attention, and attention drives learning. According to Sylwester, the arts are the "handmaiden" to this process (31). Multiple intelligence activities require students to use their artistic expression. Marion Diamond (D'Arcangelo 1998) reminds us that repetition helps memory; presenting information over again in various ways helps memory. Such is the aim of multiple intelligence activities.

Science for Every Learner places a particular emphasis on the musical intelligence. Learning through song is fundamental to human nature. For thousands of years before writing was developed, humans passed on their accumulated cultural wisdom to the next generation through songs and chants. According to Norman Weinberger (1998), brain research shows that music is biologically rooted and fundamental to human development. In every culture, some form of music has evolved. Robert Sylwester (1998) states that our brain's language and music systems both must be developmentally stimulated: "Song uses such elements as tone, melody, harmony, and rhythm to insert important emotional overtones into a now slowed-down verbal message" (31). Like Gardner, Sylwester points out that part of our brain is set up to process music and art. These parts wouldn't be in the brain if they weren't important. We all know how easy it was to learn the alphabet with a song. Students effortlessly learn important scientific vocabulary and sequences through the songs and raps in this book and on the CD. Music and song bring both singers and listeners a sense of joy and a positive emotional connection to the subjects being learned.

National Science Education Standards

The standards emphasize the importance of teachers' "developing understanding of how students with diverse interests, abilities, and experiences make sense of scientific ideas and what a teacher does to support and guide all students" (57). The standards also speak of the importance of giving students some choice in their learning. Multiple intelligence activities allow for such diversity in students and provide them with choices.

The following chapters of this book provide models of the Format for Understanding with studies of science as inquiry, sound, electricity, living things and monarch butterflies. Try them out with your students. My hope is that your students' enthusiasm and success will inspire you to design your own studies using the Format for Understanding.

Suggestions for Multiple Intelligence Activities

 Bodily-Kinesthetic

do experiments
make inventions
perform skits
make models
use the computer

 Verbal-Linguistic

think-pair-share
write or tell a story
give an oral presentation
write poems
make metaphors or draw analogies
keep journals
learn quotations
hold debates
learn vocabulary

 Logical-Mathematical

solve problems
take measurements
search for patterns in data
draw conclusions
make a flow chart
show steps in a sequence
compare and contrast

 Musical-Rhythmic

listen to songs, raps, and musical stories
create an audiotape
collect sounds related to a subject
   (bird calls, sounds of a storm or the ocean)
create a dance (also bodily-kinesthetic)
use rhythm to aid memory
conduct scientific experiments about music and rhythm
make a musical video

 Visual-Spatial

make graphs
draw objects observed
paint murals
make posters
create Mind Maps
use graphic organizers
draw cartoons
illustrate books
use maps

 Interpersonal

make cooperative projects and presentations
ask peers to teach peers
discover together
work as a community of professionals
plan community-service projects

 Intrapersonal

think about own thinking
set goals for learning and using new material
reflect on learning

 Naturalist

apply new learning to a study of the natural world
look for patterns in the environment

Science for Every Learner, © 2000 Zephyr Press, Tucson, Arizona

Science as Inquiry
Experimenting

National Science Education Content Standards

As a result of the lessons, all students should develop

- understanding about scientific inquiry   (standard A)
- abilities necessary to do scientific inquiry   (standard A)
- understanding of science as a human endeavor   (standard G)
- understanding of the nature of science   (standard G)
- understanding of the history of science   (standard G)

The Science as Inquiry Study at a Glance

Big Questions

The essence of the study, through which all the objectives, activities, and assessments are aligned:

- What is scientific inquiry?
- How do you do an experiment?

Time Frame

Between one week and one quarter depending on your schedule and goals

Domain Matrix

A tool to check the alignment of objectives with activities and assessments (page 6)

Assessing Understanding

Portfolios and journals are ongoing projects. Think Trix questions assess student understanding and thinking skills along the way. The performance task with rubric culminates the study when students design and execute experiments of their choosing. The focus is on self *and* teacher assessment throughout the study.

Discovering the Concepts

Based on Cohen's Taxonomy for Discovery—experiencing, organizing, sharing, and processing

Laying the Foundation

Students experience various clear liquids to discover the value of making direct observations. They discuss their findings about the nature of scientific thinking and the kinds of questions it can and cannot answer.

Constructing the Learning

In groups, students collect data, organize them, and share their findings with other groups. In a class discussion, they reflect on the experiences and begin to make generalizations. Students conduct their own inquiries about paper whirligigs then organize and share their findings. Students process their experiences by noting steps they used intuitively that are part of formal scientific experiments: stating hypotheses, working with independent and dependent variables, using a control, collecting data, and writing findings.

Creating a Context for the Discoveries

The play (page 16) is about a family that uses experimenting to answer their everyday questions. The story (page 18) describes scientific thinkers who have contributed to the world.

Deepening the Learning

Multiple intelligence activities create real-world and personal connections to the material (page 20). Students use music, cooperative learning, Mind Maps, and other activities to explore scientific inquiry.

Background

In some ways the inquiry study serves as an underpinning for the rest of this book. This unit is about learning to think as scientists do—to ask questions and look for answers using scientific habits of mind.

If you ask students to draw a scientist, many will draw a funny-looking white male with wild hair, wearing a lab coat and holding a steaming test tube. This image is one that few students would want to model themselves after.

Students need a new view of scientists with more positive images so they can imagine themselves as scientists and scientific thinkers. They need to know that all kinds of people become scientists: Women are scientists. People of different races are scientists. People with disabilities are scientists.

with instruments that can increase the effectiveness of the five senses. A scientist asks questions and systematically goes about finding answers to those questions by carefully observing and investigating, and by learning about the scientific work of others. The writers of the National Science Education Standards point out that there are various types of scientific investigations:

- observing and describing objects, organisms, or events
- collecting specimens
- seeking more information
- discovering new objects and phenomena
- making models
- experimenting

Archimedes (287–212 BCE) was a Greek scientist and inventor. Once there was a question about whether or not a certain goldsmith had cheated the king. The goldsmith claimed that the crown he had made for the king was pure gold. Archimedes suspected his claim. One day, as Archimedes was stepping into the bathtub, he had a sudden inspiration. As the story goes, in his excitement, he ran naked down the street shouting, "Eureka! I found it!" Archimedes' hypothesis was that a body immersed in water displaces water equal in volume to the body. Once he had the weight and volume of the object, he was able to determine the density. The density of metals is constant. By comparing the crown's density to the density of pure gold, Archimedes was able to determine that the crown was not pure gold.

So what is a scientist? A scientist is a person who is curious. What do scientists do? They attempt to satisfy their curiosity. Learning becomes exciting for students when they, too, are given opportunities and develop tools to satisfy their own curiosity about their own questions. Nurturing students' curiosity, their spirit of inquiry, may be the key to motivation in the classroom.

Science is based on information that can be observed through the five senses alone or

In this study we focus on scientific inquiries that involve experiments. The step-by-step procedure for performing an experiment—asking a question, developing a hypothesis, observing and collecting data, and keeping a record of the process and results—is often referred to as the *scientific method.*

Some educators are leery of the term *scientific method* because they think it implies that there is only one right way to investigate something. They are concerned that their students will think of science as a mere guessing game: If students' hypotheses turn out right, they win. If the hypotheses are wrong, they lose. Or if they hypothesize something and figure out along the way that they are off track, too bad. They still have to follow the steps through to the bitter end.

The scientific method doesn't need to be a rigid process, however. As Wendy Saul (Saul and Reardon 1996) points out in *Beyond the Science Kit*, there is more to inquiry than the ability to guess one right answer. Students are motivated when they can choose to investigate questions that interest them, come up

Take the whirligig activity students do in this study. A cookbook approach would require all students to experiment with the whirligigs in the same way, with the expectation that they would all arrive at one "correct" response. In the whirligig experiment included here, students collect some data, then organize it and share the results with others. In this way, students write and talk about their own investigations and present their own procedures. The procedures become a means for students to describe, clarify, make connections, and build concepts rather than an end in themselves.

Albert Einstein had a highly developed imagination. It is said that one day, he was daydreaming in a field. As the sun filtered through his eyelashes, he imagined riding on a beam of light. Later, he translated the insight that came from this reverie into a mathematical formula, which became the basis for his theory of relativity. Many people have tested Einstein's hypothesis against observable data. So far, they have found that Einstein's hypothesis fits the data better than previous hypotheses.

with hypotheses about the answers to the questions, then have the flexibility to revise their hypotheses if their investigation leads them to. When students realize they have made mistakes, they begin to observe more carefully and control variables more rigorously. As they consider their findings, they may need to rethink their experimenting to follow a different path from their original one. This trial-and-error approach enables students to develop real habits of scientific thought.

This approach is in direct contrast to the cookbook approach that teachers traditionally have used to teach science. The cookbook approach requires students simply to follow the steps of an experiment devised by someone else. Cookbook investigations teach students that if they follow the directions carefully enough, they will get the correct result. This approach teaches students that science is about procedures and getting the right answer; the mystery and fun of science are lost. In real scientific inquiry the focus is more on curiosity than procedures.

Inquiry science works best when there is time for students to explore the subject or material freely, without a focused problem or investigation. Eventually, students need to describe their investigative experiments in great detail and with great accuracy to ensure they can be replicated to verify the results. In this study the whirligig activity follows the steps of the Taxonomy for Discovery. Students freely explore with the whirligigs at first.

Good science learning needs to have three elements:

- It must engage students in real scientific problem solving, not just in following recipes.

- It must be relevant to the students' own experience and environment.

- It must be rigorous, requiring students to question, find patterns, compare, disagree, revise, and plan just as scientists do.

Scientific inquiry starts with explorations that lead to observations that lead to questions. A question leads to a hypothesis, an educated guess. Verifying the hypothesis, finding out if it is true or not, takes systematic inquiry—the scientific method.

There are a variety of ways to come up with a hypothesis. In the whirligig example, the free exploration and observation lead students to develop hypotheses based on experience that students then test for themselves. Hypotheses can also arise from hunches, intuition, and accidents.

The stories about Archimedes and Einstein illustrate that scientific inquiry is not necessarily a dull, plodding, linear process. It can involve great intuitive leaps.

You can help students move from their first spark of curiosity to formulating hypotheses and experimental designs to test the hypotheses by asking the following questions:

- What do we want to find out?
- How can we make the most accurate observations? What tools might help us?
- Is this the best way to answer our questions?
- If we do this, then what do we think will happen?

- What data would answer that question?
- What are the best observations or measurements to make?
- How do we organize the data to present the clearest answer to our questions?
- How many times should our test be repeated?

As students move through the Discovering the Concepts phase of each unit, hypotheses are likely to emerge naturally from their investigations. Students will begin to find patterns in the data that they will want to test further. These patterns will be the basis for their hypotheses. In addition to the hypotheses, aspects of scientific inquiry you will want to discuss with your students include the importance of observing systematically, measuring accurately, controlling variables, and comparing their ideas with those in current scientific thinking.

Students' understanding of these concepts can help them become discerning and responsible citizens, whether in simply reading the paper or deciding how to vote. A maxim for scientific inquiry is "Never take anything on faith: Check it out for yourself!"

Domain Matrix

The domain matrix is a tool to help you assess the alignment between stated objectives and activities. You may want to add other objectives to those I have included to suit your own class. You might include, for example, objectives in other subjects or social skills, such as leadership and cooperation. Adapt the activities to help you achieve those objectives. For more information about domain matrices, see page viii.

Activities and Assessments	Outcomes and Objectives					
	Research	Scientific Inquiry	Problem Solving	Teamwork	Nature of Science	Habits of Mind
Discovering	X	X	X	X	X	X
Plays and Stories	X	X			X	X
MI Activities	X	X	X	X	X	X
Think Trix	X	X	X		X	X
Journal	X	X	X	X	X	X
Portfolio	X	X	X	X	X	X
Performance Task	X	X	X	X	X	X

Objectives

- Students will begin to understand the nature of science, its strengths and limitations
- Students will develop scientific habits of mind, including openness to new ideas, healthy skepticism, and discernment about scientific claims
- Students will learn to formulate hypotheses and systematically test them
- Students will develop problem-solving skills
- Students will develop teamwork skills
- Students will develop the ability to experiment with skill

Activities and Assessments

- Experiences that raise questions and feed discussions about the nature and modes of science
- Examinations of components of scientific inquiry—the *whats, whys,* and *hows*
- A story and play to put the discoveries that students make into a larger context
- Multiple intelligence activities to deepen understanding
- Think Trix questions to encourage students to think about the issues
- Journals to record students' findings and reflections
- Portfolios to collect students' work and reflections throughout the study
- Performance task to answer relevant questions in students' lives

Getting Ready

- A week or two before beginning, post related words and pictures around the room (see the glossary, page 26). They will pique students' interest and prepare them for new information.

- In their journals, students make Mind Maps of what they know about scientific inquiry. At the end of the unit, they Mind Map what they have learned, then compare the two maps. Mind Mapping instructions are on page x.

Assessing Understanding

Accurate assessment of student learning is ongoing and derived from multiple sources. The following products add to students' learning as well as measure it.

Think Trix for the Science as Inquiry Study

The following Think Trix questions are examples of the kinds of questions you and your students can use to stimulate different levels of thinking. Formulate and ask these types of questions throughout the unit. Use the icons as reminders to cover each kind of question. See page xii for more information.

Recall
- What steps do you follow in an experiment?

Cause and Effect
- What are possible effects of changing more than one variable at a time?

Difference
- In what ways do dependent and independent variables differ?

Similarity
- A scientific experiment is like a _____ because _____.

Idea to Example
- Explain two methods for testing a claim that one brand of tissues is stronger than its competitors.

Example to Idea
- This statement is an example of which step in an experiment: "A paperclip added to my whirligig will make it turn faster"?

Evaluation
- What do you think are some of the most important ways that science has helped us? How did you make your choices?

Journal

A journal is usually a written collection of reflections. However, journals can also include lists of data that students have collected, the organization of those data, drawings, songs, and other entries.

Journaling is one way for students to self-assess, giving them opportunities to integrate, synthesize, evaluate, and reflect on learning. Here are some ideas of what students can do in their journals.

- Mind Map (see Getting Ready, page 7)
- Keep records of their personal inquiries. What questions come up in the study? How can they find answers? What do they observe? Discuss? What experiments do they do? What research sources do they use?
- Record what they learn in a science log. What do they understand that they didn't before? Which aspects of this subject do they feel they understand? What have they learned about themselves as learners?
- Establish connections between this study and other science studies or other subjects they have studied.
- Note the aspects they don't understand and their next steps for learning about those aspects.

Ask students to respond to the following in their journals:

- A problem I have with doing experiments is _____.
  One way to solve this problem is _____.
- If I could be any famous scientist, I would like to be _____
  because _____.
- Something in science I am curious to know more about is _____.
- One way I could find out more is _____.

Portfolio Possibilities

A portfolio is a collection of student work that provides evidence of growth of knowledge, skills, and attitudes. Portfolios provide a systematic and organized way for students and teachers to collect and review evidence of student learning over time. A key component of portfolios is a reflection page to go with each entry and with the portfolio as a whole. For more information on portfolios, see page xii. Ask students to include any or all of the following in their inquiry portfolios:

- Records of experiments and other lab reports
- Reflections on experiments and labs, including parts of work with which they are especially pleased, parts they would do differently another time, and possible implications of their findings
- Mind Maps
- Written preparation for debate on a scientific issue
- Songs they have composed related to scientific inquiry
- List of advertiser's claims, with each labeled testable or not testable
- Answers to Think Trix questions
- Self-assessments, peer assessments, teacher assessments

Discovering the Concepts

The activities guide students to discover the concepts. More about this phase and a constructivist approach to learning is on page xiv. This chart shows the steps for the Taxonomy for Discovery. These steps structure the unit for true discovery. A rubric for the taxonomy is on page 148.

Experiencing	Organizing	Sharing	Processing
Investigate. Make observations. Collect data.	Make charts, graphs. Look for patterns.	Compare observations with those of other groups.	What did we learn?

Laying the Foundation

Students need to understand the need for experimentation. This activity or one like it can serve as a springboard for delving further into experimentation.

A Demonstration to Introduce the Need for Experimentation

Objectives

- Students begin to discover the value of making direct observations.
- Students begin to practice the skills involved in the Taxonomy for Discovery—experimenting, organizing, sharing, and processing.
- Students begin to develop hypotheses based on observations.
- Students begin to explore the nature of scientific thinking, including the kinds of questions science can deal with (the processing phase in the Taxonomy for Discovery).

Materials

▶ 3 or 4 identical glasses or test tubes

▶ equal amounts of various clear liquids such as white vinegar, flat lemon-lime soda, diluted ammonia, and water to go in each

▶ plastic wrap to cover each glass

Procedure

Step 1. Pour a different clear liquid into each jar, and mark it 1, 2, or 3.

Step 2. Show the class the containers and ask them to guess what liquid is in each by looking only (most assume it is water).

Step 3. Ask students to vote on what they think is in each jar. Write down the results of the vote.

Step 4. Ask if voting is an effective way to determine what the liquids in the glasses are.

Step 5. Introduce the Taxonomy for Discovery by guiding students through the following stages:

Experiencing: Ask students, "What might be some better ways to tell what the liquids are?" Students might respond that they can use their senses to experience the liquids. Be sure to supervise students so they take all necessary safety precautions while they observe, smell, touch, and move the liquids. Remind them that it is dangerous to taste unknown substances.

Organizing: Students individually choose ways to organize their observations. They might, for instance, choose to fill in a matrix such as the one below. It will be more valuable for students to organize their observations in their own ways rather than asking them to organize it in your way. They can check their organizational method against this chart.

	Jar 1	Jar 2	Jar 3
Look			
Smell			
Feel			

Sharing: Invite students to share their findings in small groups so they can see that there are many right ways to organize information. If you show students the matrix after they have designed their own ways to organize their data, ask them to compare the two systems, noting the advantages and disadvantages of each.

Processing: Ask students if they would like to revise their original hypotheses (guesses about the liquids). Ask them to recall the steps that led them to revise their guesses. Discuss the value of observation and data collection in improving guesses. Explain that experimentation involves a systematic way to observe, hypothesize, collect data, and reach logical conclusions about something. Ask students to list ways they experiment and use other types of scientific inquiry in their lives; for example, when they try to figure out why a lamp won't light.

In the organizing stage, students determine how well the data "fits" the hypothesis—and find out the results. Next, the sharing and processing stages come into play. Students share the results of their experiments with one another.

Finally, in a class discussion, students process their findings. You can provide the vocabulary words to help them name their discoveries where appropriate. If you had presented this material in a lecture, it may not have had much meaning for your students. But because you have given students the opportunity to construct their own meanings from their discoveries, they have many hooks to connect the input to what they already have discovered. Discuss with students ways that scientific thinking is different from other kinds of thinking. Brainstorm aspects of life that can and cannot be tested with science.

This liquids activity or one like it can serve as a springboard for delving further into experimentation. Constructing the Learning adds some important aspects to the concept of experimentation.

Constructing the Learning

Investigating Whirligigs

Objectives

- Students develop their skills used in the Taxonomy for Discovery: observing, collecting data, writing down findings, organizing those findings, communicating their findings to others, developing strong hypotheses.
- Students understand the relationship between independent and dependent variables.
- Students discover the necessity of testing one variable at a time.

Materials

▶ copy of whirligig pattern and directions for each student

▶ copy of variable sheet for each student

▶ scissors

▶ paper clips

▶ timers (optional)

▶ crayons (optional)

Procedure

Step 1. Pass out the whirligig pattern, instructions, and scissors. Ask students to follow the instructions to make the whirligigs or lead them through the process, if necessary.

Step 2. Guide students through the stages of the Taxonomy for Discovery.

Experiencing: Students freely experience the whirligigs, then they write down their observations. Students find out as much as they can about what whirligigs can do, trying the following and noting their findings.

- Students hold the whirligigs as high as possible above their heads and drop them.
- Students stand on chairs or at the top of a staircase and drop their whirligigs.
- Students add weight to their whirligigs by attaching paper clips or other objects, change the direction in which they fold the blades, or color each blade a different color. They note how the variations affect the ways in which the whirligig falls—the number of twirls, the time it takes for them to reach the ground, the direction in which they twirl. They may come up with other things to compare.
- As students investigate the whirligigs, ask them what they need to do to keep the tests fair. Students of all ages understand the concept of fairness, and it is a natural way to introduce the idea of variables and controlling them.

Organizing: Students find a way to organize their data—charts, graphs, or other graphic organizers.

Sharing: Small groups share the procedures and results by answering the following questions:

- What did students find out?
- What did they do to make sure their tests were fair?

If there are disagreements, students experiment again.

Processing: Students share their findings with the class, including the following points:

- Guesses about how the whirligig will behave are *hypotheses*.
- Collecting quantifiable data—data with numbers—makes it easier for others to confirm results.
- Variables, such as the height from which the whirligig is dropped or the number of weights on it, affect the behavior of the whirligig.
- Changing one variable at a time makes the test more "fair," or accurate.
- Writing down results is important.
- To test a hypothesis, such as that a paper clip on the bottom of a whirligig will make it spin more times before reaching the ground, students need a control experiment—one in which everything but the variable remains the same.

Photocopy page 15, "Thinking about the Whirligig," for students. Help them understand the relationships between dependent and independent variables:

Step 1. List independent variables (variables the experimenter can manipulate) that could affect the whirligig's performance—size, kind of paper used, height from which it is dropped.

Step 2. List possible ways the variables will affect the whirligig's performance—make it twirl faster, slower, not at all; reach the floor more quickly. These differences are dependent variables because they are dependent on the independent variables.

Step 3. With students, look for possible relationships between the independent and dependent variables. Which variables have a direct relationship (as the independent variable is increased, the dependent variable increases)? Groups of students agree on a way to construct a line graph that shows a direct relationship (the line within the axes travels from the lower left to the upper right; see below.)

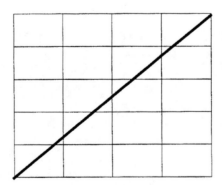

The first level of the Taxonomy for Discovery leads students to develop strong hypotheses. Students can use the Science Experiment Sheet (page 14) to test their hypotheses. Notice that the Science Experiment Sheet has the conventional scientific method steps: hypothesis, procedure, results, and conclusion. Make multiple copies of this sheet so students can record their experiments with whirligigs and other experiments that interest them. Students may also find the Science Experiment Sheet helpful when they do the Accidental Science Performance Task.

Whirligig Template and Instructions

Materials

- whirligig template
- various weights of paper
- scissors
- paper clips
- tape (optional for experimentation)
- markers (optional for experimentation)

Procedure

Step 1. Cut out the strip.

Step 2. Cut along the dotted lines above part X and part Z.

Step 3. Fold part X behind part Y along the solid line.

Step 4. Fold part Z behind part Y along the solid line.

Step 5. Fold part W behind part Y along the solid line. You might paper-clip the fold.

Step 6. Cut along the dotted line between the sun and the moon. Fold the blade with the moon in one direction and the blade with the sun in the opposite direction (see diagram).

Step 7. Experiment with the whirligig by dropping it from various heights, coloring the blades, using various weights of paper to make your whirligig, adding paper clips or other weights. Note how the changes affect the way in which your whirligig drops.

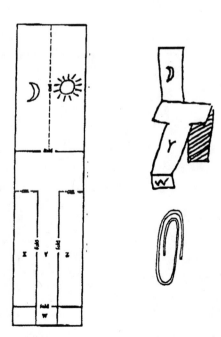

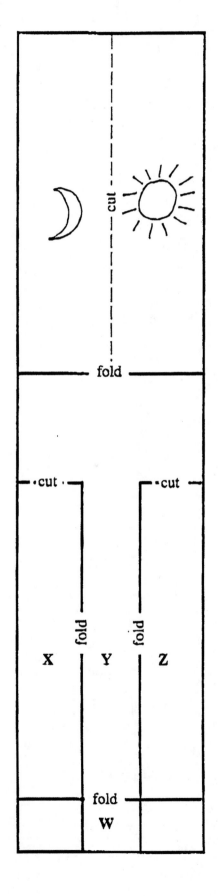

Name _____ Date _____

Science Experiment Sheet

Background _____

_____

_____

_____

_____

Hypothesis: I think that if _____

_____

_____

then _____

_____

_____

_____

_____

Equipment _____

_____

_____

_____

Procedure _____

_____

_____

_____

_____

Variables I will keep constant are _____

_____

_____

The one variable I will change is _____

Results: (My graph and data chart are attached.)

Conclusion _____

_____

_____

Possible further experimentation _____

_____

_____

References _____

_____

Science for Every Learner, © 2000 Zephyr Press, Tucson, Arizona

Thinking about the Whirligig

Next to each number, list something you think will change the way the whirligig behaves—a heavier paper, the height at which you launch it, and so on. These changes are called *independent variables*.

1. _____
2. _____
3. _____
4. _____
5. _____
6. _____
7. _____
8. _____
9. _____
10. _____

Next to the corresponding number below, list ways you think the whirligig's behavior will be affected by that change—twirl faster, spin in the opposite direction, and so on. These changes are *dependent variables* because they depend on the independent variables.

1. _____
2. _____
3. _____
4. _____
5. _____
6. _____
7. _____
8. _____
9. _____
10. _____

Creating a Context for the Discoveries

Play: Experimenting

The play gives a big picture overview of the subject matter, including relevant issues and important vocabulary and concepts without a lecture. Page xx has more information about plays. This play is on the CD. Ask students to consider these questions:

- How does the Variable family experiment to answer questions in everyday life? What sequence of actions do they suggest for doing an experiment? What questions do you have that you could test?

Cast: Narrator, Valerie Variable (Vinny's big sister), Mom Variable, Dad Variable, Vinny Variable (an eight-year-old child)

Narrator: Scene 1—The Variable family comes to the breakfast table.

Valerie: Mommmm! Vinny spilled his milk again all over the floor—and he didn't clean it up!

Vinny: I did, too! I cleaned it up with this paper towel.

Mom: Looks like you need to use a quicker picker-upper, Vinny.

Dad: Mmmmm, been watching too much TV, honey?

Vinny: I will, Mom. Hmmm. I wonder if this paper towel really is the quicker picker-upper?

Dad: You could *test* it, you know. Get a piece of each brand of paper towel. Then time how long it takes for each brand to pick up the same size spill. Keeping them the same size is controlling a variable.

Valerie: Dad's right, Vinny. *Controlling variables* is what you do to keep the test fair. And give it some *trials,* repeat the test a bunch of times, so you know your results aren't just an accident.

Vinny: You think you're so smart just 'cause you're in high school.

Mom: Well, you do learn a few things there. Wait a minute; does this experiment mean Vinny is supposed to spill more milk?

Vinny: Sure, Mom! For the sake of science! Okay, everybody. Time me. Here I go. One, two, three. Look! This one is the quicker picker-upper. Yesss!

Mom: Grmmmm. All right, Vinny. You'd better get the rest of that mess cleaned up.

Vinny: It says here on the box that this is the cereal kids love best. I don't believe it.

Valerie: Vinny! You knocked over the cereal box!

Dad: Oh, good. Now he can eat his whole breakfast off the floor!

Mom: No harm done. We'll just clean it up. See, Vinny. It's good that you don't believe everything you read. You have a *hypothesis*, a guess, that their claim is wrong. You could test your guess—at least with the kids you know. Get a group of kids . . .

Vinny: You mean, like my friends Tyrone and Jeremy?

Dad: Well, you may want a larger *sample* than that, say, all the students in your class.

Vinny: I get it. Then get different kinds of cereal and find out which one they love best.

Valerie: You catch on quick for such a young kid. And you could graph your data to show how many kids loved each kind of cereal best. Keep a record of what you did and how you did it in a book.

(Bird sound—Tweet, tweet.)

Mom: There goes that canary, Tweety, again. Mmm, I got her some new food. I don't think she likes it as much as the old food.

Vinny: Hey, Mom. You could do an *experiment* to find out! Yeah!

Mom: Right, Vinny. I could *measure* the same amount of food in each feeder, alternate the place I put them—to control the variables and make it fair—then measure how much is left . . .

Valerie: But first you may want to do some *research,* Mom. Get some books and articles and read about what canaries like to eat from some different sources, not just from the manufacturers.

Vinny: You better have a bunch of trials. Try it for some days. Tweety may just need to get used to the new stuff.

Dad: These are good ideas, but we need to get going if we want Vinny and Valerie to be on time for school and for us to be on time for work.

Mom: Maybe I'll start my experiment tonight.

Narrator: Scene 2—In the car.

(Sounds of traffic)

Valerie: Vinny! Get on your own side!

Vinny: Okay, okay. Gimme a break . . . Hey, Val. There are experiments we could do with the car.

Valerie: You mean like how long your sister can put up with your elbow in her ribs?

Mom: Now, now, Valerie. Vinny just likes being with you. Speaking of experiments, we could test and see which route to school is the fastest and which gas gets the best mileage.

Dad: The gas mileage could help me with my research. I'm doing a study to find out if it would be cheaper to take our family vacation at King's Dominion or Hershey Park. One thing I'll need to know is the cost of gas per mile with this car.

Vinny: Yeeeah! I love amusement parks!

Mom: We certainly don't need any experiments to find that out!

Valerie: Usually, when you go on amusement park rides, your hair gets all messed up, right? I could do an experiment to find out which hair gel keeps my hair in place better.

Mom: Well, Val, you will have to *define* what *better* means and come up with a way to *measure* any difference you might find.

Valerie: Oh, I hadn't thought of that.

Dad: You've been quiet for a while, Vinny. It's refreshing, but a little worrisome somehow.

Vinny: Yeah, Dad. It's because I've been thinking . . . You know, if I *did* test that paper towel and it *was* quicker than one other brand—or even *five* other brands—that wouldn't prove it would pick up quicker than *all* paper towels.

Dad: You are thinking, aren't you? That's right, Vinny. That's the nature of *scientific inquiry.*

Valerie: You can never know for absolute sure that no other towel in the world is as quick.

Mom: Scientific knowing is not like knowing two plus two makes four. *Scientific knowing is what you know until you find out differently.*

Dad: It sure is useful, though. Even in our everyday lives, scientific thinking means that we don't automatically have to believe everything we read or are told.

Vinny: Cool, Dad. Does that mean that I don't have to automatically believe you and Mom?

Valerie: Vinny! You're impossible!

Mom: Hey, let's try an experiment. Let's see if it's possible for you two to be nice to each other for the rest of this ride.

Vinny: Remember, Mom. You'd have to define what *nice* means!

Dad: My hypothesis is that the Variable family would enjoy some peace and quiet!

Story: The Scientific Method through History

You may tell stories with rich sensory descriptions and as if the students were actually in the story. Such techniques can help students develop their ability to make internal visual images, which is useful for mathematical thinking and problem solving in general. Stories provide another way to reinforce vocabulary and concepts. Page xx has more information about stories.

The scientific method as we know it began more than four hundred years ago in Italy. At that time people began to ask testable questions, make systematic observations, and collect data to answer their questions. People began to write down their findings and share them with a community of others who were interested in the same questions. Members of the community could perform the same experiments to confirm or deny the results. They could also build on the work of those who came before them and perform new experiments, answering new questions about the world.

Now sit back and relax. As you take in a deep breath, use your imagination to travel back in time and space. Pretend you are Galileo Galilei. It is the late 1500s. To those around you, authorities decide what is true and not true. You have a different idea, though. You find that if you make observations and perform experiments, you can answer questions for yourself.

Up until now, everyone has agreed with the philosopher Aristotle that heavy objects fall faster than light objects. You decide to test this idea. One day, as the story goes, you climb up to the top of the leaning tower of Pisa. Look down on the plaza far below you. Choose two objects of different weights. To control variables, make sure the objects are made of the same materials. Feel the heavy object in your left hand and the lighter object in your right hand. See and hear the people looking up at you. Now drop the objects. Look! Listen! They land at the same time. Now write down your findings so that other people can find out whether they get the same results.

Your unusual approaches for answering your questions will get you in some trouble down the road. But you have started a new way of thinking that will change the world.

Ask a testable question. Test it. Observe and collect data—numbers are important. Write it all down. In this way other people can build on your work.

In 1642, the year Galileo died, the great scientist Isaac Newton was born in England. Now become Isaac Newton. You are fascinated by the writings of Galileo. Now use his ways of testing to make many discoveries yourself. Here is an example: One day you perform a test to find out more about light. Put a light behind a glass prism. Look at the beautiful colors on the other side of the prism—red, orange, yellow, green, blue, violet. It's a rainbow! Now pick up a tool and carefully measure the angle for each color. Write down your findings. People around you don't believe that white light is made of colors. But in time, other scientists test light the same way you did and confirm your results. Eventually the world comes to agree that white light is made of all the colors of the rainbow.

Now it is 1746. You are a British doctor, Charles Lind. For some years now, ships have been sailing all over the world. Many sailors on these ships, though, have been getting sick with a disease called scurvy. What causes the disease and, more importantly, what can cure it? You will answer this question using scientific thinking. You pick twelve sailors with scurvy and systematically test six possible cures: cider, oranges, lemons, vinegar, seawater, and a nutmeg mixture. To control variables, you have them all eat the same thing otherwise. Your experiment shows that only oranges and lemons cure scurvy. This discovery will save thousands of lives. Later researchers will find through new controlled experiments that it is the vitamin C in the citrus fruits that the sailors need to stay healthy.

Let's move forward in time. You come into the world in 1867 and your name is George Washington Carver. Born a slave, you will become a great scientist someday. Even as a little child you have a way with plants. Imagine gently touching a plant right now. Look, smell, feel the plant. You just seem to know what it needs to grow well. Young as you are, people call you the plant doctor. When you grow up, you combine this understanding with scientific thinking to make great discoveries. Imagine working tirelessly in your laboratory at Tuskeegee University, testing your hypotheses, your guesses about how to make new products. Your experiments bring about hundreds of new uses for peanuts, sweet potatoes, and soybeans. Your work helps farmers all over the southern part of the United States.

Now, imagine traveling to the other side of the world. You are a brilliant young scientist named Marie Curie. You were born in Poland in 1867. Now you live in Paris and are systematically studying the properties of radiation in a mineral called *pitchblende.* Look at the dark material. It feels like tar, doesn't it? Test the material. Over and over you dissolve the pitchblende, then make it solid again, patiently trying to find what causes the radiation. Finally you discover an element you name *radium.* You will receive two Nobel Prizes for your scientific work. Radiotherapy, made possible by your experiments, will be used to help people overcome cancer.

Come forward now in time all the way to the present day. Imagine being yourself, performing an experiment. You have a hypothesis, a guess about what will happen in the experiment, just like the scientists before you. You control the variables, just like they did. You write down your data so that others may know what you did.

You are working in the same way as scientists all over the world who continue to use the scientific method in their experiments. Thousands of journals publish their findings so other scientists in their community can confirm or question the results. In this way scientific understanding about the world grows and grows.

Deepening the Learning

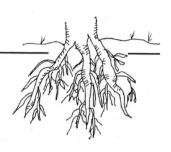

Multiple Intelligence Activities

Use a multiple intelligence approach to give students opportunities to develop more links in the brain for deeper understanding and greater emotional ties to the new learning. As students develop real-world connections and practice applying the new knowledge in a variety of circumstances, they enhance their ability to transfer their learning to new situations.

Interpersonal

- Students find out as much about the history of their school as they can. Based on this experience, they brainstorm the various ways to do research. Students can apply these research skills to scientific investigations.

- In groups of four, students choose scientific words on the wall or in handouts. The groups take turns defining words and asking for help defining or understanding words they don't know.

- Students take part in round-table cooperative learning: three or four students pass a piece of paper among themselves, and each lists examples of instruments used to enhance the five senses in investigations (for example, thermometers, microscopes, telescopes, CAT scans). Groups take turns sharing from their lists.

Logical-Mathematical

- Discuss the importance of writing exact procedures so that someone else can replicate an experiment.

- Students write very specific instructions for making a peanut butter and jelly sandwich. Another student follows the directions as written. For example, if the writer says spread the peanut butter on the bread, but doesn't say to use a knife, then the one who follows the directions must use fingers. The results can be hilarious! Discuss the importance of being very exact when writing the procedure so that someone else can replicate the experiment.

- In small groups, students list questions that can be investigated scientifically and those that cannot.

Visual-Spatial

- Students Mind Map the most important elements of an experiment.

- Students make a graph that shows changes in their stress levels throughout the semester. Students discuss the value of graphical presentations of data.

- Using the lyrics from the "Scientific Method Blues" or a song of their own, students create an illustrated book for younger students about how to conduct an experiment.

Verbal-Linguistic

- Students use flash cards to learn scientific terminology.
- Students debate an ethical issue that has arisen as a result of scientific experimentation; for example, cloning.

Intrapersonal

- Students list advertisers' claims and analyze them. Which claims could be tested using the scientific method? Students decide which claims they could test themselves and how they could do it.

Bodily-Kinesthetic

- Students design and execute as many experiments as possible.
- Students create and take part in a role-play in which the characters are personifications of components of the scientific method; one player acts as the hypothesis, another player acts as the procedure, and so on. Through the role-play, the players reflect their characters' contributions to scientific experiments.

Naturalist

- Students take part in investigations about living things in their backyards or school yards. See "Living Things Study" and "Monarch Study" for more ideas.

Musical-Rhythmic

- Students write songs about various scientists and their contributions.
- Students design experiments that involve music, such as recording the various pitches made by striking glasses with various amounts of water in them, or comparing the distances from which people of various ages can hear a sound. See the "Sound Study" for more ideas.

Scientific Method Blues

Use this song from the CD to teach the steps and vocabulary in experiments. See page 158 for the musical score and page 178 for the dance steps.

If you have a question
You want to test,
You've got to make your
Hypothesis.

For your *guess* to be smart,
Gotta do your part;
Get the *research*
before you start.

Refrain:

Oh, the Scientific Method,
It's the way to go, yes it is.
Yes, the Scientific Method.
If you want to show what you know.

And now you're set
To design your *test*.
Change one *variable*;
Control the rest.

Then you get your *data*
(That's numbers to you).
Repeat the trials.
Make sure they're true.

Refrain

Keep a *record*,
Keep it in a *book*.
If anyone asks you,
Say, "Take a look!"

And make a *graph*,
The *results* to cite.
Then draw the *conclusions*.
Were you wrong or right?

New Refrain:

Oh, it really doesn't matter,
You just want to know.
Right or wrong is not the question.
You just want to show what you know.
Ooh, yeah! That's right!

Words by Kathleen Carroll. Music traditional. Singer and guitar, Joe Brady; guitar, Ollie Harma; harmonica, Jon Michael Carroll.

Performance Task for Science as Inquiry

Performance tasks are products or performances you can use to assess student understanding. Understanding, in this sense, means the ability to apply facts, concepts, or skills to new situations. With performance tasks, the assessment is embedded in the product or performance itself. Use the Science Experiment Sheet (page 14) to help students organize their experiments.

Accidental Science

Background

You have been helping one another design and perform scientific experiments.

Task

Design an experiment to answer a question that comes up in your daily life: "Which dog food does my dog prefer?" "Can my friends really tell the difference between Pepsi and Coca Cola?" "Which route to school is the fastest?" "What change in my daily routine could make me more efficient?"

Goal

To understand that learning the scientific method and applying it in your daily life can be useful in finding out answers for and about yourself

Procedure

Step 1. Choose a testable question.

Step 2. Research to find out what is already known or claimed to be known about the question.

Step 3. Design an experimentation plan.

Step 4. Check out your plans with critical friends, then with your teacher. Does your plan need to be revised?

Step 5. Conduct the experiment, controlling the variables.

Step 6. Write down the experiment and the results.

Step 7. Organize the data in a graph or table.

Step 8. Share your results and your conclusions.

Format adapted from "A Teacher's Guide to Performance-Based Learning and Assessment" (1996) and teachers of Connecticut's Pomraug School District 15.

Rubric

*A rubric provides criteria and standards for assessing a student's learning. A rubric also serves as a self-assessment tool for the students to use while designing the product or creating the performance. A rubric makes it possible for peers, teachers, and the students themselves to easily calculate a numerical score that represents the quality of the student's performance. **For more information about how to score the rubrics, please refer to number 5 on page xvi.***

Performance Rubric for Experimental Design

Criteria	Advanced	Intermediate	Beginner
Hypothesis Formulation	Testable hypothesis based on research in alignment with the experiment's design.	Experiment tests the hypothesis; some research evident; lack of clarity in the design.	Experiment does not test the hypothesis; no research evident.
Variables	Experimenter manipulates only one variable; all others remain constant.	Experimenter manipulates one variable; most others remain constant.	Experimenter manipulates more than one variable.
Data Presentation	Accurate data with appropriate repetition of trials presented in clearly labeled graph or table.	Accurate data; presentation may need improvement, or more trials may be needed.	Data insufficient, inaccurate, or non-existent; or presentation lacks organization.
Conclusion	Logical response to hypothesis based on collected data.	Responds to the hypothesis; data could have been analyzed more thoroughly.	No conclusion, or conclusion not based on data or not related to hypothesis.
Clarity	Written procedure thorough enough for others to replicate experiment.	Procedure can be followed accurately with the help of a few additional directions.	Procedure unclear.
Completeness	All components clearly recorded.	Most components clearly recorded.	Major components are lacking.
Creativity	New research.	Innovative demonstration of established fact.	Demonstration taken from a book.

Extensions

Sometimes students' questions take them beyond their ability to observe and experiment directly. The World Wide Web and student trade books offer ideal opportunities for students and teachers to extend their research, often leading to new and better questions, observations, and experiments.

Web Addresses

www.sln.org

This ideal inquiry Web site for the Franklin Institute Science Museum in Philadelphia also links to other science museums around the world.

www.fi.edu

This ask-an-expert service through Franklin Institute Science Museum allows your students to ask questions of science experts.

www.learningteam.org

This site has Find it! Science: The Books You Need at Lightning Speed. Also available through CD-ROM, it offers detailed descriptions of hundreds of science trade books.

Book Corner

Books related to the study can do much to spark student inquiry. In addition to science books, include biographies, fiction, poetry, dictionaries, encyclopedias, and other types. Create a center in the classroom with books, pictures, photographs, magazines, and CDs. Here are a few possibilities:

Dash, Joan. 1990. *The Triumph of Discovery: Women Scientists Who Won the Nobel Prize.* Englewood Cliffs, N.J.: Julian Messner.

Only ten of more than five hundred Nobel Prize winners in science were women. This book tells about the great contributions of and the obstacles overcome by four of them.

Ingram, Jay. 1992. *Real Life Science: Top Scientists Present Amazing Activities Any Kid Can Do.* Toronto, Can.: Greey de Pencier Books.

An anthropologist shows students how to research their families as she does orangutans in the wild. Makes use of astronomy, zoology, food science, and psychology, and includes easy-to-use materials.

Ipsen, David. 1988. *Archimedes: Greatest Scientist of the Ancient World.* Hillside, N.J.: Enslow.

Details Archimedes' contributions to astronomy, physics, mathematics, and engineering. Provides special insight into ways Archimedes used reasoning to solve problems.

Kramer, Stephen. 1987. *How to Think Like a Scientist: Answering Questions by the Scientific Method.* New York: HarperCollins Children's Books.

Amusing black-and-white drawings show how scientific procedures can be used to answer questions every day.

McKissack, Patricia. 1994. *African-American Scientists.* Brookfield, Conn.: Milbrook Press.

Outlines the lives of several African American scientists: Benjamin Banneker, George Washington Carver, Percy Julian, and Shirley Ann Jackson. Informative photographs and drawings.

Glossary

An important part of science literacy is learning the language of science. Classrooms with posted words, stories, and games make learning vocabulary easy and fun.

conclusion: a judgment reached by reasoning and based on the results of an experiment

control: a sample used for comparison in an experiment

data: facts or figures from which conclusions can be drawn

dependent variables: a quantity or thing that changes when the independent variable changes; the change is dependent on the independent variable.

experiment: an investigation performed to test a hypothesis

graph: a diagram that shows the relationships between sets of items

hypothesis: a good guess made as a starting point for investigation

independent variable: a quantity, thing, or action that the experimenter changes

measure: to find out a quantity of something by comparing it to a unit of known size

observe: to use one's senses to discover information about something

record: to put down in writing for future use

research: to investigate carefully

sample: a small part intended to show what the whole is like

systematic: according to a plan or system

trials: tests

variables: a quantity, thing, or action that can change

Teacher Reflection

There is no need for teachers to know all the answers. One of the best things you can do for students is to serve as a model of a life-long learner. Use this reflection page to record some of your new understandings as you complete this unit.

What are some of your new understandings in regard to teaching and learning about this subject?

What in this unit worked for your students?

What were some problems that arose?

How could you overcome those problems next time?

What are some other things you would like to remind yourself about this study for next time?

Sound Study

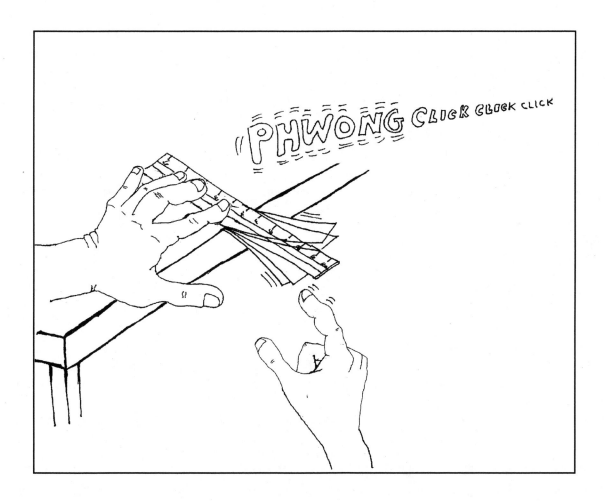

National Science Education Content Standards

As a result of the activities, all students should develop

- ◾ abilities necessary to do scientific inquiry   (standard A)
- ◾ understanding of the characteristics of sound,
  a form of energy   (standard B)
- ◾ understanding of the characteristics of organisms   (standard C)
- ◾ understanding of the structure and function of living things   (standard C)
- ◾ abilities of technological design   (standard E)

The Sound Study at a Glance

Big Questions

The essence of the study, through which all the objectives, activities, and assessments are aligned:

- What is sound?
- How do we hear?

Time Frame

Between one week and one quarter depending on your schedule and goals

Domain Matrix

A tool to check the alignment of objectives with activities and assessments (page 32).

Assessing Understanding

Portfolios and journals are ongoing projects. Think Trix questions assess student understanding and thinking skills along the way. The performance task with rubric culminates the study when students make their own musical instruments. The focus is on self *and* teacher assessment throughout the study.

Discovering the Concepts

Based on Cohen's Taxonomy for Discovery—experiencing, organizing, sharing, and processing

Laying a Foundation

Experiences through which students understand basic ideas about vibration and pitch

Constructing the Learning

Students move from station to station, examining the properties of sound with tuning forks, cup-and-string telephones, dry rice jumping on the speaker of a CD player, bottles containing various amounts of water, and other materials. Student groups collect data about sound from each station, organize the data, and share their findings with other groups. In a class discussion, they reflect on the experiences and begin to make generalizations.

Creating a Context for the Discoveries

The play (page 44) describes how a sound forms and moves through the ear. In the story, students go to an imaginary musical performance where they actually see and feel the sound waves coming out of the instruments (page 46).

Deepening the Learning

Multiple intelligence activities create real-world and personal connections to the material (page 47). Students record an imaginary interview with a sound wave, solve mathematical problems involving the frequencies of notes, draw to music, and create a dance to a rap.

Background

This study reaches four different areas of the National Science Education Content Standards. It helps students develop inquiry skills (standard A). While sound waves are invisible, the movements of objects that cause sound waves are visible. And changes in pitch and loudness are audible. Work with sound naturally leads students to new questions, many of which can be answered by direct observation and experiment.

As students discover more and more about what sound is (standard B), they may ask themselves, "How do we hear sounds?" This study also addresses how sounds move through various parts of the ear and eventually to the brain (standard C). Finally, the performance task, making a musical instrument, introduces technology as a part of sound (standard E).

Sound is a kind of energy. Sound waves form when an object moves or vibrates. The back and forth vibration of an object, say a guitar string, moves the air around it, which produces sound waves that radiate in every direction. We usually think of sound waves moving through air. In addition to air, though, sound waves move through other materials, such as water or metal. Unlike light waves, which can move in a vacuum, sound waves always need to move through a medium. Sound travels much more slowly than does light, which is why we hear thunder after we see lightning.

Sound waves can travel in different frequencies. *Frequency* refers to the number of cycles or humps of a wave per unit of time. These frequencies correspond to differences in pitch. The humps of low-pitched waves are spread farther apart than high-pitched waves. Objects with more mass have lower pitch; that is, they make deeper sounds than objects with less mass. That is why the larger, thicker vocal cords of a man make sound waves with a lower frequency and pitch than the small vocal cords of a boy. Differences in mass also explain why large drums have deeper tones than small drums. Sound waves can also differ in amplitude, which is the size of the wave. Differences in amplitude correspond to differences in loudness.

The outer ear serves as a funnel to catch sound waves. The waves move down the ear canal and vibrate the eardrum. The vibrations are amplified by three little bones—the hammer, the anvil, and the stirrup—collectively known as *ossicles*. The ossicles send the sound waves to the inner ear. The sound waves pass into a liquid-filled tube in the shape of a snail shell called the cochlea. Semicircular canals, which help people keep their balance, are attached to the cochlea. The cochlea has hairlike cells that pick up the vibrations and transmit them to the auditory nerve. The auditory nerve carries the sound as an electrical impulse to the brain.

When students make their musical instruments in the performance task, they follow the five stages of technological design put forth in the National Science Education Contents Standards: They (1) state the problem, (2) design an approach, (3) implement a solution, (4) evaluate the solution, and (5) communicate the problem, design, and solution.

Domain Matrix

The domain matrix is a tool to help you assess the alignment between stated objectives and activities. You may want to add other objectives to those I have included to suit your own class. You might include, for example, objectives in other subjects or social skills, such as leadership and cooperation. Adapt the activities to help you achieve those objectives. For more information about domain matrices, see page viii.

Activities and Assessments	Outcomes and Objectives							
	Research	Scientific Inquiry	Problem Solving	Teamwork	Vibration	Sound Waves	Loudness or Pitch	Hearing
Discovering	X	X	X	X	X	X	X	X
Plays and Stories					X	X	X	X
MI Activities	X	X	X	X	X	X	X	X
Think Trix					X	X	X	X
Journal	X	X	X	X	X	X	X	X
Portfolio	X	X	X	X	X	X	X	X
Performance Task	X	X	X	X	X	X	X	X

Objectives

- Students will develop skills in scientific inquiry, problem solving, teamwork, and technology
- Students will communicate effectively about a technological problem and solution
- Students will understand vibration, the movement that produces sound
- Students will understand sound waves and the media through which they travel
- Students will understand the relationship of loudness to the amplitude of sound waves
- Students will understand pitch, which affects the frequency of sound waves
- Students will understand hearing, and the structure and function of the ear

Activities and Assessments

- Hands-on experiences to produce sound with a variety of materials
- Story and play to put the discoveries students make into a larger context
- Multiple intelligence activities to deepen understanding
- Think Trix questions to encourage students to think about the issues
- Journals to record students' findings and reflections
- Portfolios to collect students' work and reflections throughout the study
- Performance task to demonstrate understanding using musical instruments

Getting Ready

- A week or two before beginning, post related words and pictures around the room (see the glossary, page 53). They will pique students' interest and prepare them for new information.

- In their journals, students Mind Map what they already know about sound. At the end of the unit, they Mind Map what they have learned, then compare the two maps. Mind Mapping instructions are on page x.

Assessing Understanding

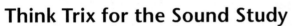

Accurate assessment of student learning is ongoing and derived from multiple sources. The following products add to students' learning as well as measuring it.

Think Trix for the Sound Study

The following Think Trix questions are examples of the kinds of questions you and your students can use to stimulate different levels of thinking. Formulate and ask these types of questions throughout the unit. Use the icons as reminders to cover each kind of question. See page xii for more information.

Recall

- Study the picture of the ear and its parts below; then draw and label your own picture without looking at the original.

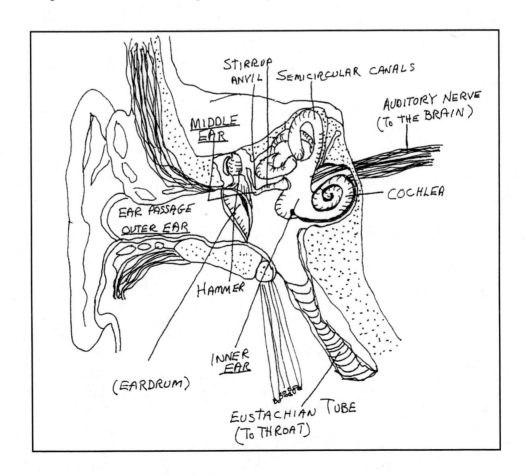

- If you hold a string up to your ear tightly and pluck it, what effect will lengthening the string have on the pitch of the sound you produce?

Difference

- What are some differences in the sound you produce when you tap on a jar containing water and when you blow into that same jar?
- How might sound waves that come from random noise differ from those that come from music?

Similarity

- In what ways are the sounds a person's vocal cords produce similar to the sounds a guitar produces?
- Someone throws a pebble into a still pool of water. How are the waves on the surface of the water similar to sound waves?

Idea to Example

- Give an example of a musical instrument that uses a wooden box to amplify or increase the loudness of its sounds.
- A student is plucking a rubber band. Describe one way she could raise the pitch of the rubber band.
- Sound travels through string more clearly than through the air. Describe an activity that would prove that this statement is true.

Example to Idea

- Why does a big drum make a lower pitch than a small drum, and a thick string make a lower pitch than a thin string?
- What do a guitar string, a person's voice box, and a piano key have in common?

Evaluation

- Which musical instrument would you rather be, a drum or a flute? Why?

Journal

A journal is usually a written collection of reflections. However, journals can also include drawings, songs, and other entries.

Journaling is one way for students to self-assess, giving them opportunities to integrate, synthesize, evaluate, and reflect on learning. Here are some ideas of what students can do in their journals.

- Mind Map (see Getting Ready, page 33)
- Keep records of their personal inquiries. What questions come up in the study? How can they find answers? What do they observe? Discuss? What experiments do they do? What research sources do they use?
- Record what they learn as in a science log. What do they understand that they didn't before? Which aspects of this subject do they feel they understand? What have they learned about themselves as learners?

- Establish connections between this study and other science studies or other subjects they have studied.
- Note the aspects they don't understand and their next steps for learning about those aspects.

Ask students to respond to the following:

- The thing I like most about my instrument is . . .
- The most frustrating thing about making my instrument was . . .
- Some of my favorite sounds are . . . because . . .
- Some sounds I don't like are . . . because . . .
- If I could be an expert player of any musical instrument just by wishing, it would be . . . because . . .

Portfolio Possibilities

A portfolio is a collection of student work that provides evidence of growth of knowledge, skills, and attitudes. Portfolios provide a systematic and organized way for students and teachers to collect and review evidence of student learning over time. A key component of portfolios is a reflection page to go with each entry and with the portfolio as a whole. For more information on portfolios, see page xii. Ask students to include any or all of the following in their sound portfolios:

- Favorite work from the journal, including Mind Maps, data collection and organization from the discovery stations, various inquiries and research
- CD of the radio interview with the sound wave, and the sounds the student CDd with the explanations for them
- CDs of students' own songs and raps about sound
- Students' paintings to different kinds of music
- Drawing or photograph of three-dimensional model of the ear
- Drawing, writings, and photographs of the musical instrument the student made
- Flow chart that describes the path of a sound wave from its source to the brain
- Drawings and comments about the instrumental pieces
- Experiments students designed and performed in relation to their questions about sound
- VideoCD of students' dances
- Responses to Think Trix questions
- Students' written plans for the performance task
- Video- or CD of the students' presentations for the performance task
- Students' reflections about the performance task, new understandings, successes, and ways to improve

Discovering the Concepts

The activities guide students to discover the concepts. More about this phase and a constructivist approach to learning is on page xiv. This chart shows the steps for the Taxonomy for Discovery. These steps structure the unit for true discovery. A rubric for the taxonomy is on page 148.

Experiencing	**Organizing**	**Sharing**	**Processing**
Investigate. Make observations. Collect data.	Make charts, graphs. Look for patterns.	Compare observations with those of other groups.	What did we learn?

Laying the Foundation

Students need to understand certain foundational concepts as they begin a study of sound. These include the notions that (1) sound comes through movement; (2) the back and forth movement that produces sound is called *vibration*; and (3) by changing the ways that vibrations are made, we can change the pitch of a sound. Following is an activity that uses the four stages of Cohen's Taxonomy to help students begin to understand these concepts:

What Is Sound? An Introduction

Objectives

- Students discover that sound occurs through movement.
- Students discover that the back-and-forth movement that produces sound is called a *vibration*.
- Students learn that by changing the ways that vibrations are made, they can change the pitch of a sound.
- Students continue to develop skill in making observations, collecting and organizing data, communicating findings to others (experiencing, organizing, sharing, and processing in Cohen's Taxonomy for Discovery), and reflecting on the process.

Materials

▶ a wood or plastic ruler for each student

Procedure

Step 1. Pass out a ruler to each student.

Step 2. Guide students through the four stages of Cohen's Taxonomy for Discovery.

Experiencing: Students use all their senses to carefully observe sounds as they are made. Students hold one end of the ruler on the table or desk with the other end extending beyond the edge. They push on the extended end with their hands, letting the end go suddenly, and observe the results. Next, students experiment by extending more and less of the ruler beyond the edge of the desk, striking the edge as described earlier. They note which lengths produce a high pitch and which produce a low pitch. They record their findings.

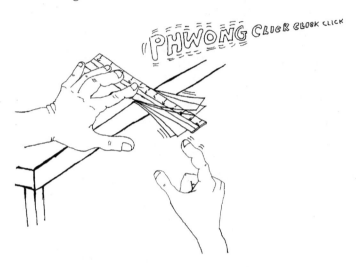

Organizing: Students organize their findings in a chart or graph. Following is one possible way to graph the findings:

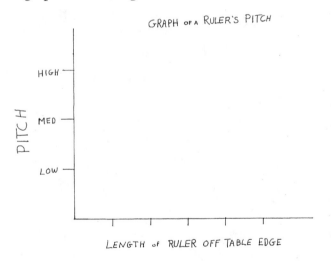

Sharing: Students share their findings in small groups.

Processing: The class discusses their findings. The following concepts should be included:

- For there to be a sound, something has to move.
- The movement has a name: *vibration*. Students can see the ruler vibrate as it makes a sound.
- The greater the length of the ruler extending beyond the edge of the desk, the lower the pitch.

Constructing the Learning

The goal of these activities is to give students a number of experiences with sound. Through these experiences, students will have opportunities to develop their own understanding about the nature of sound. The sections suggest options for setting up stations about sound, followed by reproducible directions for each station and for using the taxonomy with the stations:

Sound Experiments

Objectives

- Students will reinforce the idea that sound comes from movement, that the movement is called a *vibration,* and that they can change the pitch of a sound by changing the ways the vibrations are made.

- Students will understand that sound travels more effectively in a confined space than in an open space.

- Students will see that the greater the mass of an object, the lower the pitch of sound it produces; the lesser the mass, the higher the pitch.

- Differences in loudness of sounds are due to differences in the size, or amplitude, of sound waves.

Materials

▶ See individual experiments.

Procedure

Step 1. Read through the materials required for each station. Feel free to duplicate the station directions. (Laminating or placing the directions in sheet protectors can prolong their life.) Put the materials and directions for each station in a different place. Have enough chairs at each station for all group members.

Step 2. Set up the stations on students' desks and give students about five minutes at each station. As an alternative, set up semipermanent stations in the classroom for the duration of the study of sound. In this case, students try to reflect on the activities as they have time.

Step 3. Tell students that they will be making observations and writing them down as they perform the activities at each station. Later they will organize the data and compare their findings with those of other groups.

Step 4. Ask students to designate pages in their journals for observations and reflections about each station. The journal entries will provide the basis for a discussion and comparison of the groups' results.

Step 5. Ask students to participate in the stations, using the four stages of Cohen's Taxonomy as outlined below.

Experiencing:

- Doing—Members of each group work with the materials at each station.

- Observing—Students make observations about what happens.

- Writing—Students may be so involved that you need to remind them to record their findings. They collect and record their observations based on the questions asked at each station as well as on their own inquiries.

Organizing: Groups of students come up with a way to organize their observations. Students look for patterns or similarities among the data they collect at the stations with regard to vibration, loudness, and pitch. They may use tables, charts, or lists to organize their data, or they may choose some other method. Within groups, students discuss what the patterns reveal.

Sharing: Groups of students compare the patterns they found with those of other groups. They look for observations that do not match, then cooperate to design an investigation to test their contradicting hypotheses. Groups may decide to go back to a particular station and retest the materials to resolve their differences.

Processing: In the class discussion that follows the activities, make sure the following concepts are included:

- Whenever a sound occurs, something has to move.
- The movement is a back-and-forth motion called a *vibration*.
- Vibrations are visible.
- Invisible sound waves are in the air.
- Sound travels more effectively in a confined space than in an open space.
- Sounds are high or low, which is pitch. This corresponds to the difference in frequency of sound waves.
- Objects with greater mass produce a lower pitch; objects with less mass produce a higher pitch.
- Sounds are loud or soft. Differences in loudness correspond to differences in the sizes of sound waves.

Station 1: Seeing and Feeling Sound Waves

Materials

▶ tuning forks (several, in different keys, if possible)
▶ a clear glass bowl
▶ water

Procedure

Step 1. Strike the tuning fork against a desk or table.

Step 2. Put it close to your ear.

Step 3. Put the vibrating fork against your skin. How does it feel?

Step 4. Put the vibrating tuning fork in the water. What happens? Why?

Step 5. What else can you find out about sound at this station? Write down all your discoveries.

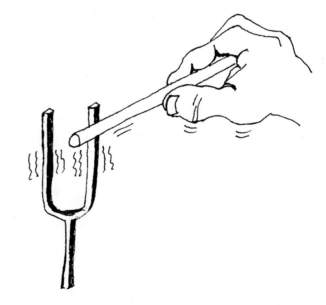

Station 2: Observing Sound Travel through Solids

Materials

▶ polystyrene and paper cups

▶ various types of string and cord, each piece seven to ten meters long

▶ paper clips

▶ Cup-and-string telephones may already be at this station for you to use.

Procedure

Step 1. Make a hole in the bottom of each cup at the center.

Step 2. Thread an end of the string through each hole.

Step 3. Tie a paper clip to the end of the string on the inside of the cup to keep the string in place.

Step 4. Hold the cup to your ear without touching the string.

Step 5. Ask a classmate to do the same with the other cup, keeping the string as taut as possible without breaking the bottom of the cup.

Step 6. Take turns talking into the cup and listening.

Step 7. Ask a third student to watch the string carefully. What does he or she see when you talk?

Step 8. Ask the student to pinch the string while you talk. What happens? Why?

Step 9. Record what else you find out at this station.

Station 3: Observing Effects of Loud and Soft Sounds

Materials

▶ aluminum pie pan

▶ uncooked rice

▶ a CD player

▶ a CD of music

▶ red marker

▶ blue marker

▶ a CD of a person speaking

Procedure

Step 1. Pour some rice into the aluminum pie pan and place the pan on the speaker of the CD player.

Step 2. Play the music and turn the volume up. Use the red marker to draw what the rice looks like.

Step 3. Turn the volume down. Use the blue marker to draw what the rice looks like now.

Step 4. Record what you think the differences in your pictures show.

Step 5. Repeat the experiment with a CD of speaking. Does the rice look different than it did when you played music?

Step 6. Record the other findings you discovered at this station.

Station 4: Vibration and Pitch—Wind Instruments

Materials

- ▶ five or six identical bottles with narrow mouths
- ▶ a ruler for tapping them
- ▶ a container of water

Procedure

Step 1. Do some experiments with these materials. Tap and blow into the bottles, noting the various sounds that containers with various amounts of water in them make.

Step 2. What can you find out about vibration and pitch? Pitch is how high or low a sound is. Write down what you notice about the sounds. Explain why you think you got the results you did.

Step 3. Try to play a song with these materials. Write down what you do. Record what you find out.

Step 4. Record the other findings you discover at this station.

Station 5: Vibration and Pitch—Stringed Instruments

Materials

- ▶ several pieces of string made of differing materials, each about a meter long
- ▶ one piece of string with the handle of a spoon tied to its middle (see illustration)

Procedure

Step 1. Put a piece of string to your ear. Hold the other end taut with the thumb and middle finger of your other hand.

Step 2. Pluck the string with your index finger. Experiment with trying to make the pitch higher and lower.

Step 3. Write down your findings.

Step 4. Use your fingers to hold the ends of the string with the spoon to your ears.

Step 5. Hit the spoon hard against a desk or chair.

Step 6. What does the spoon sound like? Write it down.

Step 7. Why do you think it sounds like that? Write down your ideas.

Step 8. Record your other findings at this station.

Station 6: Vibration and Pitch—Percussion Instruments

Materials

- ▶ nails of various lengths
- ▶ a ruler
- ▶ a spoon
- ▶ optional: blocks of wood
- ▶ optional: hammers

Procedure

Step 1. Lay several nails loose on the desk.

Step 2. Put your head close to the desk and tap each nail with the ruler or spoon.

Step 3. Note which nails have the highest and lowest pitches, and record your findings.

Step 4. Record why you think the different nails produce different sounds.

Step 5. Hammer some nails into the wooden block.

Step 6. Note which nails have the highest and lowest pitches and record your findings.

Step 7. Record why you think the different nails produce different sounds.

Step 8. Record any additional findings from this station.

Possible Findings at Station 1: Seeing and Feeling Sound Waves

The vibrating tuning fork makes a long-lasting sound that slowly fades. The vibrating movement tickles the skin. When placed in the water, the fork makes a surprising splash. Students will be able to see the patterns in the water caused by the moving tuning fork if you place the bowl on an overhead projector and screen.

Possible Findings at Station 2: Observing Sound Travel through Solids

The students talking with each other on the telephone will notice that the sound travels better through the string than in the open air. This is because the waves spread out in the open air, but they are confined in the string. If a student spoke into a garden hose, the voice would be VERY loud at the other end. In this case, the sound would travel through air, but the air is confined.

The vibration from the student's vocal cords make the air in the cup vibrate. The cup transfers the vibration to the string and on to the other cup. The air in the other cup reproduces the exact vibrations. In this way, the second student hears the first student's voice right in the cup she is holding. The cup-and-string telephone can transfer a whisper that may not be heard through the air. Some types of cups may amplify the sound more effectively than other types. The third student can actually observe the vibration of the string as the other two talk. If anyone touches the string, the vibration will be stopped. This activity demonstrates that sound occurs only when something moves. When the vibration stops, the sound stops. It also demonstrates the fact that materials vary in their ability to carry sound.

Possible Findings at Station 3: Observing the Effects of Loud and Soft Sounds

This activity makes the effect of sound waves visible. Loud sounds have greater amplitude than soft sounds. When the volume is turned up, the vibrating rice jumps higher than when the volume is low.

Possible Findings at Station 4: Vibration and Pitch—Wind Instruments

The glass with a small amount of water will produce the highest sound when tapped. The glass with the most water will produce the lowest sound.

Students may be surprised to notice that the opposite is true if they blow over the mouths of the bottles. The bottle with the most water will have the highest sound; the bottles with the least water will have the lowest sound.

Both effects can be explained by the same principle: the greater the mass of the material that vibrates, the lower the pitch of the vibration. When the whole bottle is tapped, the lower vibration comes from the bottle with the greatest mass (that is, the most water).

The bottle with the least water has the longest column of air. When someone blows into the bottle, only the long column of air vibrates, not the rest of the bottle. In this case the bottle with the longest column of air has the greatest mass vibrating and will produce the lowest pitch. Likewise, with harmonicas, wind instruments with long columns of air produce low notes; those with short columns produce high notes.

Possible Findings at Station 5: Vibration and Pitch—Stringed Instruments

Strings made of different materials will produce somewhat different sounds. All the strings, however, will produce a low pitch when the taut part of the string is long and a high pitch when the taut part of the string is short, another example of the principle that the greater the mass of the material that vibrates, the lower the pitch. With musical instruments, the strings made of thick material produce a lower pitch. Strings made of thin material produce a higher pitch.

The sound waves travel more efficiently through string than through the air. Sound heard through the string is louder than sound heard through the air. The string with the spoon in the middle gives an even more dramatic demonstration of this fact than the string alone. When you hit the spoon and listen through the string, the spoon sounds like a loud, bellowing church bell. Spoons (and hangers) made of various materials produce different sounds. Silver spoons provide the purest and most beautiful sounds.

Possible Findings at Station 6: Vibration and Pitch—Percussion Instruments

The nails with the most mass give the lowest pitch, again demonstrating the principle described above. Consider different-sized drums. All things being equal, large drums will have a lower pitch than small drums.

The wooden table or desk amplifies the sound made by the nails because the whole desktop vibrates with the nails. Many musical instruments, such as pianos and guitars, use wooden boxes to amplify the sound, or make it louder.

Creating a Context for the Discoveries

BIG
PICTURE

Play: The Autobiography of a Sound Wave

The play gives a big picture overview of the subject matter, including relevant issues and important vocabulary and concepts without a lecture. Page xx has more information about plays. This play is on the CD. Ask students to consider these questions:

- What is sound? How do sound waves move? How do loudness and pitch affect sound waves? How do sound waves move through the ear to the brain?

Cast: Susie Sound Wave, Salvadore Sound Wave

Susie: Hello, my name is Susie Sound Wave and I've got a story for you to hear! So please turn your ears on and listen.

It starts at the beginning—my birth! Remember when somebody stuck a ruler over a desk and hit it with their hand so that it moved up and down? Wrrrrrrrrrrr.

(Make a ruler sound.) Tha-a-at wa-as when I was bor-rn just as the ruler was dancing up and down. That up and down movement is called *vibration*. **Remember, to have a sound, something has to move! To have a sound, something has to move! To have a sound, something has to move!**

I moved out in a wave into the air around the dancing ruler. You know how air moves when you fan your face? Like that. (Echoing vibration in the background) I began to grow and spread wider and wider as the air moving next to the vibrating ruler started pushing on the air next to it, which pushed on the air next to it, and so on. You guessed it! That moving air is called a *sound wave*! Of course, we sound waves can move through other things besides air—like wood, metal, and even water!

There are other ways we can be born, too. Meet my brother, Salvadore Sound Wave.

Salvadore: (Deep loud voice) Hello. One day some guy started yelling, vibrating those little strings in his *voice box* called *vocal cords*. As his vocal cords began to shake, so did the air around them, and I was born! Feel your own throat and say, "Ahhhhhh." Can you feel your vocal cords vibrate?

Susie: Look, you just made our cousins. There are Sarah, Sam, and Stacey Sound Wave!

Salvadore: Now I, Salvadore Sound Wave, am a *taller* sound wave than my sister, Susie, because the sound that made me was *louder*. (Make a loud sound.) I also move *slower* than Susie because my sound has a *lower pitch*. (Make a low sound.) I move like a pole-vaulter; my waves are large and slow.

Susie: I move like a sprinter; my waves are small and fast!

Salvadore: Feel your throat and make a loud sound, then a soft sound. Do they feel different? Make a high-pitched sound, like this, "eeeeeeeeeeeee." Now make a low-pitched sound, like this, "ooooooooooo." They don't feel the same either, do they?

When you put a little bit of a ruler off a desk and pluck it, the ruler makes a high pitch, right? You can make the pitch lower by lengthening the amount of ruler hanging off of the desk.

Salvadore and Susie: The more the mass that makes the sound, the lower the pitch. The more the mass that makes the sound, the lower the pitch. The more the mass that makes the sound, the lower the pitch.

Salvadore: Obviously, I must have come from more mass than Susie.

(Change the sounds from high pitch to low.)

Susie: So much for my brother. Now back to my story. Get ready! The real adventure begins when I hit those funny-looking, crinkled things on the outside of your head—I believe you humans call them ears. I don't blame you for trying to dress them up with rings and things, but it doesn't help much, if you want my opinion. But funny looking or not, those outer ears do get the job done. They catch us sound waves so we can continue our trip. Whee, here I go—into the ear!

Here comes the ear canal—you know, that's the place where you are never supposed to put anything smaller than your elbow (unless it happens to be us sound waves)! I'm sliding down your ear canal like it's a slide at the water park to the middle ear with its eardrum. Boy, it's fun to vibrate that eardrum! Whooey!

(Drum sound)

From the eardrum I go on to vibrate three little bones: I shake through the hammer, hit the anvil, which shakes the stirrup and moves me to the inner ear. What a ride in the inner ear—just like a roller coaster! (Music that goes around and around) I can go round and round in the fluid in the semicircular canals (which help people with balance, by the way) and into the cochlea. The cochlea is like a snail shell. Moving through the smooth, soft hairs inside, I play them like a piano. (Piano sounds)

Watch those hairs vibrate. Now they are sending messages through your auditory nerve to your brain. All this lets you know the sound wave's loudness and pitch and, for voices, whose voice the sound wave belongs to. The brain knows the difference between Susie and Salvadore Sound Wave.

So, how is that for an adventure? My life is pretty useful to you, isn't it? By the way, if you want to tell your own story, you'll need my help. I'll carry the sound to your listeners.

Salvadore: Or perhaps I will.

(Closing music)

Science for Every Learner, © 2000 Zephyr Press, Tucson, Arizona

Story: An Evening of Music—with a Difference!

> *You may tell stories with rich sensory descriptions and as if the students were actually in the story. Such techniques can help students develop their ability to make internal visual images, which is useful for mathematical thinking and problem solving in general. Stories provide another way to reinforce vocabulary and concepts. For more information about stories, refer to page xx.*

Take in a deep breath and, in your mind's eye, pretend it is evening and you are walking into a large room. Take a seat along with the rest of the audience. Watch the musicians in the orchestra on the stage as they tune up their instruments. Notice something peculiar? You can actually see and feel the sound waves coming out of the instruments! Watch the colorful waves come out from the strings of the violins, from the openings in the flutes, from the mouths of the horns. Right now, as the players first begin to tune up, the waves are coming out every which way. The colors are clashing. See the waves zigging, zagging, and bumping into each other. The waves look like people wandering in different directions in a street, some of them even fighting. This is noise or cacophony. Cacophony means bad sound. The noise feels sharp against your skin, doesn't it?

Look! Now the instruments are coming into tune with each other. The sound waves are becoming orderly as if the wandering people are beginning to march in step in a parade! We are beginning to have symphony—where the instruments come together to make harmonious sounds. The colors are making beautiful patterns. Yes, here comes the music! At first it's loud. The music is vibrating your whole body! See the bright, intense colors coming out of the orchestra. Then the music changes and becomes much quieter. Now the colors are pale pastels, and the music feels more like a gentle tingle.

Look at the drummer play that large kettle-drum. The pitch is low. The frequency is low. See, the humps are far apart. You can feel those low sounds in your legs and stomach. What colors do you see with the low notes? Now the drummer hits on a smaller drum. Notice, the pitch is higher; the frequency is higher. See, the humps are close together. A higher frequency makes a higher-pitched sound. High-pitched sounds feel more like a tickle on your head and shoulders. What colors do you see now?

Check out the stringed instruments. When the violinists move their bows across the bigger, thicker strings, the waves are spread out, and the frequency and pitch are low. You see it again with the flute. See the flute players put their fingers over the low note? The column of air is long, and the pitch is low. Watch and feel those spread-out sound waves flow out of the flute. As always, the more the mass that makes the sound, the lower the pitch.

Look at how the sound waves from the orchestra are harmonizing! The vibrations surround you like a gentle hug. The waves are making beautiful, orderly patterns, sometimes bright and colorful, sometimes pale. They glide across the room and slide down the ears of the audience. Relax for a bit and enjoy the sights, sounds, and feel of the music.

Now, make yourself small and follow some sound waves from the outer ear down the ear canal. Watch the sound waves vibrate the eardrum. You are in the middle ear. On you go to the three little bones—the hammer, the anvil, and the stirrup. Watch the vibration move from one bone to the next. Now you are in the inner ear. Watch the sound wave move the snail shell–like cochlea with its little hair cells. See the hair cells send the sound into the auditory nerve and up to the brain. That person is smiling because the music sounds good to the brain!

Now head back to your seat and become your regular size again. Oh, the sound waves are fading, becoming paler and paler, and the music is slowly coming to an end. Look, feel, and listen to those last few lovely notes.

Now it is time to leave the orchestra and bring your awareness back into the classroom. Remember though, you can enjoy beautiful music in your own imagination, whenever you need to take a break!

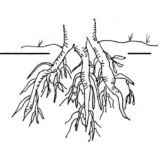

Deepening the Learning

Multiple Intelligence Activities

Use a multiple intelligence approach to give students opportunities to develop more links in the brain for deeper understanding and greater emotional ties to the new learning. As students develop real-world connections and practice applying the new knowledge in a variety of circumstances, they enhance their ability to transfer their learning to new situations.

Verbal-Linguistic

- One student pretends to be a radio interviewer. Another student pretends to be a sound wave. The interview includes the birth and adventures of the sound wave as it moves from its source to the brain of the listener.

Logical-Mathematical

- Students make a flow chart that shows the path of a sound from its source, through the air into the ear, and to the brain.

- The frequency of the musical note C is 256 Hertz (Hz). This means that there are 256 cycles per second. The frequency of the note G is 384 Hz. Both notes have overtones, quieter waves that are made at the same time as the main note. These include overtones with frequencies two times and three times the frequency of the main note. If students multiply the frequencies for the musical notes C and G by two and three, they can see why C and G sound good together. (Both notes have the same overtone, 786 Hz. Notes that have the same overtone are pleasing to the ear when played together.)

Visual-Spatial

- Students listen to a variety of instrumental music (symphony, jazz, Indian sitar, or Peruvian flute). They draw or paint a picture as they listen to each piece of music. They compare the pictures of each piece of music with the corresponding pictures by other students. They look for what the pictures have in common. Do the pictures show similarities in the ways the different musical pieces affected the students? Grouping pictures around the name of the music with student comments would make a very effective bulletin board.

- Students make and label a three-dimensional model of the ear.

Bodily-Kinesthetic

- Students take turns acting out the play, using the vocabulary name cards you provide. Role-playing the movement of the sound wave can help students become familiar with the parts of the ear as well as with the sequence of movements within the ear as it processes a sound.

Interpersonal

- Groups of students design and carry out experiments based on questions that may have arisen in the Discovery section. Following are some examples of questions they might want to investigate:

  Does the quality of sound transmission improve if you vary the type or size of the material in the cup-and-string telephone?

  Can pitch be changed by changing the water level in a bottle, the length of a ruler extended over a desk, the stretch of a rubber band, or the length of a string held up to the ear?

Intrapersonal

- Students consider the health issues involved in listening to music at high decibel levels. Is the enjoyment gained from listening to very loud music worth the loss of hearing that accompanies it? Students justify their response.

Musical-Rhythmic

- The rap in this unit can be used to create a dance. Students can make their arms move like sound waves.

- Students use the rap to make a memory map that helps them remember words and the sequence of sound movements. They might trace how the sound moves from a person's voice, through the air, to someone's ear, and to the brain.

- Students make their own raps or songs about sound.

Naturalist

- Students go outside and stand very still with their eyes closed. They each hold up one finger of their left hand for every natural sound they hear. They hold up one finger of their right hand for each mechanical sound they hear. Students open their eyes and discuss their observations.

Vibration Rap

As you listen to this song, follow the path of a vibration from its source through the ear. How do pitch and loudness affect vibrations?

Vibration is moving back and forth.
Vibration is moving back and forth.
Bells or birds or whispered words from moving vocal cords.
Vibration is moving back and forth.

Some sound waves were heard one day when someone used their voice.
They shook the air first here, then there, and the ear—it had no choice!
Well, the waves went in and caused a din vibrating your eardrum.
Then three small bones picked up the drone and shook up—every one!

Refrain

Vibration is moving back and forth. It is, ya'll.
Vibration is moving back and forth.
Bells or birds or whispered words from moving vocal cords.
Vibration is moving back and forth.

Vibration—moving back and forth;
Vibration—moving back and forth,
moving—back and forth, back and forth.
Vibrations ride through things with tides, no matter what is said;

Moving molecules quickly then bounce inside your head.
The way came clear to the inner ear for a wild and crazy ride
Through semicircular canals* the fluid had to slide.
Then cochlea's hairs sent nerves upstairs with a message for the brain.

Your brain heard words. The words you heard were,
"Sounds, they're not the same!"
Low pitch—slow; high pitch—GO.
The frequencies aren't the same.
Soft waves are small;
loud waves are tall in the vibration game.

Refrain

*The semicircular canals are for balance, not hearing.
Words by Kathleen Carroll. Music by Shade Jenifer. Rappers: Hugh Scott and Shade Jenifer with Gwen Jenifer.

Performance Task for the Sound Study

Performance tasks are products or performances you can use to assess student understanding. Understanding, in this sense, means the ability to apply facts, concepts, or skills to new situations. With performance tasks, the assessment is embedded in the product or performance itself.

Making Musical Instruments

Background

You have been studying sound for some time.

Task

Using inexpensive and readily available materials, you'll design and make a musical instrument to perform a song for other students. Then you will explain how you made your instrument, how the instrument makes sounds, and how the listeners hear the sounds.

Audience

Other students are the audience.

Goal

To use your knowledge of sound to teach and entertain others

Procedure

Step 1.   Choose materials from which to make your instrument. You can bring materials to school from home if you wish.

Step 2.   In groups of three or four, brainstorm a list of musical instruments you could make. Include facts you know about sound and hearing, the kinds of sound you would like your instrument to make, ways you might produce the sound, and ways you might vary the pitch or loudness.

Step 3.   Make the instrument.

Step 4.   Draw a picture of the instrument you made.

Step 5.   Write a paragraph that tells how you made the instrument.

Step 6.   Write another paragraph that explains how sound waves travel from the instrument, through the air, into and through the parts of the ear to the brain.

Step 7.   Play the instrument for the class, showing where the sound is made on the instrument.

Step 8.   Describe how the sound is made.

Step 9.   Show how to change the pitch.

Step 10. Show how to make the sound louder and softer. Can you make the sound loud and soft while the pitch is high? Can you make the sound loud and soft when the pitch is low?

Format adapted from "A Teacher's Guide to Performance-Based Learning and Assessment" (1996) and teachers of Connecticut's Pomraug School District 15.

Step 11. Explain how the sound moves from the instrument, through the air, through the different parts of the ear, to a listener's brain.

Step 12. Tell the class how you made the instrument. What materials did you use? What tools? Did someone help you?

Step 13. Describe any ways you changed your original plan and why you had to make the changes.

Rubric

*A rubric provides criteria and standards for assessing a student's learning. A rubric also serves as a self-assessment tool for the students to use while designing the product or creating the performance. A rubric makes it possible for peers, teachers, and the students themselves to easily calculate a numerical score that represents the quality of the student's performance. **For more information about rubrics, refer to page xvi.***

Before students present their instruments to the whole class, allow them to present to the small group. Group members can assess themselves and each other based on the rubric. Other members of the group can suggest ways each student can improve his or her formal presentation.

Performance Rubric for Sound Study

Criteria	Expert	Intermediate	Beginner
Description	Correctly identifies the source of the sound; describes it as vibration.	Correctly identifies sound's source; does not call it a vibration.	Unable to identify source of sound.
Pitch	Correctly identifies and demonstrates high pitch and low pitch; describes high pitch as faster vibration and low pitch as slower vibration.	Correctly identifies and demonstrates high pitch and low pitch.	Confuses high and low pitch or is unable to change pitch on instrument.
Loudness	Demonstrates that loudness is changed by how hard the instrument is plucked, tapped, or blown. Can change loudness when playing high or low pitch.	Can increase or decrease loudness in one direction only (e.g., can make the sound louder only when the pitch is higher).	Does not demonstrate a change in loudness or does not describe the change.
Design	Clearly and accurately describes the making of the instrument, as well as how and why the instrument actually made is different from the original plan.	Gives an adequate description of the making of the instrument, constraints faced, and causes of the modifications made to the original plan.	Unable to describe how the instrument was made and/or how and why the instrument is different from the original plan.
Hearing	Accurately describes the sequence of a sound wave's movement, including the structures of the ear involved.	One or two parts of the sequence are left out or named incorrectly.	Unable to describe the sequence of a sound wave's movement or the structure of the ear.

Some Places to Buy Materials

► Most of the materials for this study can be obtained easily from home. You may be able to get tuning forks from the science department or music department. If necessary, tuning forks can be ordered from scientific supply companies.

Extensions

Sometimes students' questions take them beyond their ability to observe and experiment directly. The World Wide Web and student trade books offer ideal opportunities for students and teachers to extend their research, often leading to new and better questions, observations, and experiments.

Web Addresses

www.exploratorium.edu/

Activities students can do to learn more about sound. It also has a wealth of other resources for an inquiry approach to science.

www.fi.edu

Ask-an-expert service through Franklin Institute Science Museum allows you and your students to receive answers to your science questions from experts in the field.

www.learningteam.org

Has *Find it! Science: The Books You Need at Lightning Speed*, a CD-ROM with detailed descriptions of hundreds of science trade books.

Book Corner

Books related to the study can do much to spark student inquiry. In addition to science books, include biographies, fiction, poetry, dictionaries, encyclopedias, and other types. Create a center in the classroom with books, pictures, photographs, magazines, and CDs. Here are a few possibilities:

Berger, Melvin. 1989. *The Science of Music.* New York: HarperCollins Children's Books.

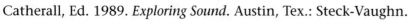

Explains how music is made. Includes instructions for making and playing one's own musical instruments.

Carroll, Kathleen. 1999. *Sing a Song of Science.* Tucson, Ariz.: Zephyr Press.

Has stories, raps, songs, activities, and Web sites about sound and pitch. Includes a CD with the story.

Catherall, Ed. 1989. *Exploring Sound.* Austin, Tex.: Steck-Vaughn.

Explores how the voice makes sound and how sound travels to the ear. Includes deafness, echoes, speed of sound, and how sound is recorded.

Kaner, Etta. 1991. *Sound Science.* San Francisco, Calif.: Perseus Press.

Describes how Beethoven, after he became deaf, put one end of a stick on a piano string and the other on his teeth. He used the feel of the vibration to determine what the note was. Includes hands-on activities to explore sound beyond those presented in this study.

Parker, Steve. 1989. *The Ear and Hearing.* Danbury, Conn.: Watts, Franklin.

Explains how the ear works using many color photographs and diagrams.

Glossary

An important part of science literacy is learning the language of science. Classrooms with posted words, stories, and games make learning vocabulary easy and fun.

auditory nerve: the nerve that sends information about sound from the cochlea in the inner ear to the brain

brain: an organ of soft nerve tissue in the skull that coordinates sensual, nervous, and intellectual activity

cochlea: the spiral, snail-like cavity in the inner ear where vibrations are turned into nerve impulses

eardrum: the membrane of the inner ear

frequency: the number of repetitions of a vibration in a given time

inner ear: the innermost part of the ear that contains the semicircular canals and cochlea

middle ear: the cavity of the central part of the ear, behind the eardrum

pitch: the highness or lowness of a tone, based on the rate of vibrations that produced it

semicircular canals: three fluid channels in the inner ear that give information to the brain to help keep balance

sound: a sensation caused in the ear by vibration in air or another medium

sound wave: a wave that passes through air or another medium

three little bones (or ossicles: the hammer, the anvil, and the stirrup): the bones in the air-filled middle ear passing vibration from the eardrum to the inner ear

vibration: the back and forth motion of a medium such as air

vocal cords: folds in the voice box vibrating an air stream to produce a voice

voice box: a hollow organ allowing an air passage to the lungs and containing the vocal cords

Teacher Reflection

There is no need for teachers to know all the answers. One of the best things you can do for students is to serve as a model of a life-long learner. Use this reflection page to record some of your new understandings as you complete this unit.

What are some of your new understandings in regard to teaching and learning about this subject?

What in this unit worked for your students?

What were some problems that arose?

How could you overcome those problems next time?

What are some other things you would like to remind yourself about this study for next time?

The Electric Study

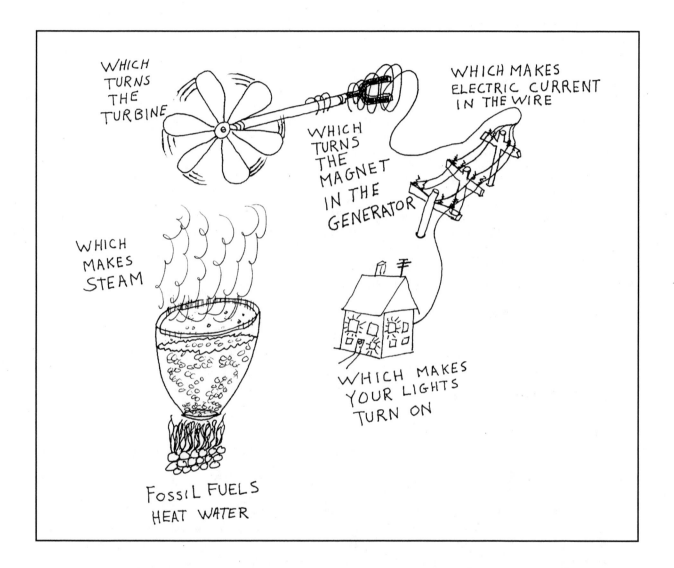

WHICH TURNS THE TURBINE

WHICH TURNS THE MAGNET IN THE GENERATOR

WHICH MAKES ELECTRIC CURRENT IN THE WIRE

WHICH MAKES STEAM

WHICH MAKES YOUR LIGHTS TURN ON

FOSSIL FUELS HEAT WATER

National Science Education Content Standards

As a result of the activities, all students should develop

- abilities necessary to do scientific inquiry   (standard A)
- an understanding of electricity   (standard B)
- an understanding of transfer of energy   (standard B)
- an understanding of science as a human endeavor   (standard G)
- an understanding of the history of science   (standard G)

The Electric Study at a Glance

Big Question

The essence of the study, through which all the objectives, activities, and assessments are aligned:

- What makes the lights go on?

Domain Matrix

A tool to check the alignment of objectives with activities and assessments (page 60)

Time Frame

Between two weeks and one semester depending on your schedule and goals

Assessing Understanding

Portfolios and journals are ongoing projects. Think Trix questions assess student understanding and thinking skills along the way. The performance task with rubric culminates the study when students explain the principles behind electrical gadgets of their own making. The focus is on self *and* teacher assessment throughout the study.

Discovering the Concepts

Based on Cohen's Taxonomy for Discovery—experiencing, organizing, sharing, and processing

Laying a Foundation

Students experience basic ideas about electricity by tinkering with small batteries, flashlight bulbs, and wire. They make the bulb light to learn fundamental information about electric circuits. They also discover which materials make good and poor conductors of electric current.

Constructing the Learning

Students use their understanding about electricity to make series and parallel circuits, and electromagnets. Then they construct gadgets of their own choosing. They learn how electrical energy is made in power plants and how it travels to their homes and schools.

Creating a Context for the Discoveries

The play (page 75) describes how particular scientists went about making the first battery, motor, generator, and other electrical inventions we depend on today. The story (page 78) focuses on the change of energy from the sun into various electricity resources such as coal, oil, and wind. It then describes the way a power plant creates electric currents from raw energy.

Deepening the Learning

Multiple intelligence activities create real-world and personal connections to the material (page 80). Students research superconductors, read meters, paint murals of a power plant, and perform the "Electric Connections Rap."

Background

Electricity is one of the strongest and most important forces in our lives. Electric energy is fundamental to life as we know it. Electric energy makes light and heat, and it makes things move. Almost every aspect of our lives, from work to entertainment and eating to temperature control and transportation, is dependent upon electric energy. This study introduces basic information on current (no pun intended) ideas about electricity and ways it is used. It also outlines the history of harnessing this source of power.

about electricity without a background in atomic theory. It may be enough to know that electric charges move in an electric current, without getting into the complexities behind electrons and atoms.

The opportunity to make electrical gadgets can motivate a variety of learners, particularly those kinesthetic students who may not excel in other academic areas. As long as you observe safety precautions, children can follow their own lines of inquiry. My students took great joy in making Morse Code trans-

All the activities, from making circuits to the final performance task, help students develop patience and perseverance, like that of Thomas Edison. Edison was attempting to find a material for the filament of light bulbs, a material that would glow when electric current was sent through it without being burnt up. As the story goes, one day Edison's assistant came into the laboratory and said, "Mr. Edison! You have tried almost 2000 materials to make a filament for your light bulb and none of them worked! When are you going to give up?" "What do you mean?" Edison replied. "I have been very successful. I now have 2000 materials I don't need to try again!" A short time later, Edison found the material for the filament for which he had been searching.

Many people have no conception about how basic things in their world operate. To them, lights go on because they flip a switch; the remote control powers the TV. Learning a few fundamentals about electric power can help students feel more connected to and make more sense of the world around them.

In order to learn about electricity, it helps for students to have some experience with magnets. If students have two small magnets to work with, they can find out for themselves that magnets have an invisible attraction for each other and for certain metals such as iron, steel, and nickel. Opposite ends of magnets attract—the North Pole attracts the South Pole. Same ends repel—the North Pole of one magnet pushes away from the North Pole of another. However, students can learn much

mitters, rigging their bedrooms with doorbells to ensure their privacy, lighting doll houses with switches and dimmers, making teaching machines—the students came up with many of these projects themselves. At times the whole classroom looked like a fix-it shop, with individuals and small groups of students happily working away on their own gadgets.

How can students come up with ideas for electric gadgets? Some students get ideas by flipping through books and magazines on electricity and electronics, others by taking apart old appliances that nobody wants anymore. Many get their ideas by seeing what other students are doing or through their own imaginations. When students are engaged in such inquiry, you don't need to know all the answers. Students become the experts about their projects, and you learn right along with the rest of your class. We also had electric fairs at the end of the study. Students showed their gadgets and inventions to students from other classes. As the visitors tried out the gadgets, the young inventors explained the scientific principles behind the gadgets.

Be sure to allow time for students to work on their projects. You might allow a half hour at the end of each day for project work, research, and independent reading. Allow students to work on their projects during free choice time as well; students frequently choose to do so because they become deeply involved.

Before beginning the projects in this unit, be sure to teach your students about safety precautions. Don't allow them to work with dangerous devices such as fluorescent bulbs, television picture tubes, microwave ovens, tube-type radios, and TV sets. Inform them that house current is extremely dangerous; they should never put anything in outlets. If students are dissecting old appliances, be sure to snip off the power cords to remove any temptation of plugging them in. Flashlight batteries are safe; car batteries are not. Avoid water. Sometimes even flashlight batteries can get hot, especially when the circuit is hooked up improperly. Instruct students to use caution when touching batteries that are hooked up.

This study offers a good opportunity to discuss the dangers of lightning, too, since lightning results from an imbalance of electric charge. Students need to know that when lightning and thunder are present, they must go indoors immediately and stay away from water. They should also refrain from using electric appliances or the telephone during electrical storms.

Students' inquiry into electricity can lead naturally to other studies of technology: computers, TVs, satellite dishes, or the space program. They delve into the issues surrounding traditional energy sources for electricity such as coal, oil, hydroelectric, and natural gas, and alternative energy sources such as wind, sun, photovoltaic, and geothermal. Some of the Web sites listed at the end of this chapter provide resources for students' special interests.

Certain terms in the study of electricity can be confusing. The term *electricity* itself can cause confusion because it has various meanings. While it may not be necessary to teach all of the definitions to young students, you may find it useful to understand the various meanings. As much as possible refer to the different aspects of electricity specifically.

- *Electric charges* are the positive and negative forces that hold matter together.
- The flow or movement of the electric charges is called *electric current*.
- *Electric energy* is the capacity to do work. It is generated by creating a flow of electric charges.

The Bicycle Chain Analogy

The bicycle chain and gears correspond to the **generator**.

This makes the push for the electric charge.

The movement of the chain corresponds to the electric current (the movement of electric charges); this moves slowly.

The distant gear corresponds to the **light** or **appliance**.

Energy for work is available almost immediately.

The links in the chain correspond to electric charges.

- The rate at which electric energy flows per second is called *electric power.*

Many elementary science books pass misconceptions about electricity on to the teachers and students. They are filled with such phrases as "flow of electric current." Bill Beaty, an expert on electricity at the science hobbyist Web site, points out that speaking of a flow of electric current is like speaking of a flow of a flow. Current is a movement, not a substance. Generators and batteries don't make electric charges. The electric charges are already in the wires. The generator or battery provides the "push" for the electric charges that are already there.

Helping students conceptualize electric current can be tricky. Beaty uses a bicycle analogy to help clarify them. He suggests that we think of an electric circuit as a bicycle chain. Each link of the chain corresponds to one electrical charge. The electric generator is like a person pushing on bicycle pedals that turn a nearby gear. The gear moves the bicycle chain. The moving chain is like the electric current.

Just as the links of the bicycle are there before anyone starts turning the pedals, in a circuit the electrons are already there before anyone connects a battery or starts cranking a generator. When an electric current is created, the circular chain of electrons goes around and around without any electrons being created or destroyed. Batteries and generators do not create electric charges, and electric appliances do not use them up.

Here's an important aspect of the analogy. Suppose we have a very long chain that is driving a distant wheel (more like a drive belt than a bicycle chain). The electric appliance, a washing machine or light bulb, for instance, is like that distant gear. What happens when the person on the pedal turns the nearby gear? The distant gear moves almost instantly (the chain is fairly tight). So how fast did the energy move? It moved almost instantly, since the whole chain moves at the same time. When he turned one gear, the other gear moved.

You might ask yourself, "How fast did one link of the metal chain move?" It moved quite slowly. Also, we can pedal the gear in either direction, making the chain move in either direction. The chain can be wiggled back and forth, yet the energy moves only in one direction, from our nearby gear to the distant gear. The energy is rapidly flowing from the nearby gear to the distant gear, regardless of which way or how fast the chain moves.

The same thing happens with electric circuits: the energy moves instantly, while the electrical current is a fairly slow-moving flow. The entire circuit is full of slow-moving electrical charges. The charges can all move in the same direction. This movement corresponds to the direct current in a battery. The charges can also move back and forth, just as our pedaling can move a bike chain back and forth. This movement corresponds to the alternating current in wall outlets.

The electrical energy, however, always flows in one direction. It starts out, say, inside the battery, and then it flows almost instantly to the light bulb—even if the wires are very long and the light bulb is a great distance from the battery. This whole process would be very confusing if we did not realize that the wires contained a long chain of charges that always move all at once, like the bicycle chain.

It is always helpful for students to see relationships between their studies. The Electric Study connects with the Living Things Study. The Sun is the source of most of the energy used to make electric power. The Living Things Study describes the Sun as the source of the energy necessary for living things to survive.

This Electric Study is a rich, relevant, and motivating source of ongoing learning for you and your students.

Domain Matrix

The domain matrix is a tool to help you assess the alignment between stated objectives and activities. You may want to add other objectives to those I have included to suit your own class. You might include, for example, objectives in other subjects or social skills, such as leadership and cooperation. Adapt the activities to help you achieve those objectives. For more information about domain matrices, see page viii.

Activities and Assessments	Outcomes and Objectives					
	Research	Scientific Inquiry	Problem Solving	Teamwork	Circuits	Electric Production
Discovery	X	X	X	X	X	X
Plays and Stories					X	X
MI Activities	X	X	X	X	X	X
Think Trix				X	X	X
Journal	X	X	X	X	X	X
Portfolio	X	X	X	X	X	X
Performance Task	X	X	X	X	X	X

Objectives

- Students will develop skills in research, scientific inquiry, problem solving, and teamwork
- Students will be able to describe open, closed, series, and parallel circuits
- Students will understand and describe materials that make good and poor conductors of electricity
- Students will understand how electricity is produced
- Students will understand the history of the use of electricity

Activities and Assessments

- Investigations with making circuits
- A story and play to put the discoveries that students make into a larger context
- Multiple intelligence activities to deepen understanding
- Think Trix questions to encourage students to think about the issues
- Journals to record students' findings and reflections
- Portfolios to collect students' work and reflections throughout the study
- Performance task to allow students to explain their understanding of electricity through the operation of their gadgets

Getting Ready

- A week or two before beginning, post related words and pictures around the room (see the glossary, page 88). They will pique students' interest and prepare them for new information.
- In their journals, students make Mind Maps of what they know about electricity. At the end of the unit, they Mind Map what they have learned, then compare the two maps. Mind Mapping instructions are on page x.

Assessing Understanding

Accurate assessment of student learning is ongoing and derived from multiple sources. The following products add to students' learning as well as measuring it.

Think Trix for the Electricity Study

The following Think Trix questions are examples of the kinds of questions you and your students can use to stimulate different levels of thinking. Formulate and ask these types of questions throughout the unit. Use the icons as reminders to cover each kind of question. See page xii for more information.

Recall

- What happens if you put the North Pole of an electromagnet to the South Pole of another magnet? What happens if two South Poles are put together?
- What is a closed circuit? What is an open circuit? What does a switch do?
- Describe the sequence in making electric energy when a power plant uses coal or oil. Describe how the sequence changes when hydroelectric power is used.

Cause and Effect

- Why is water sometimes heated in the process of making electric energy? What are some ways that the water could be heated?
- How might the environment be different if most countries used sun and wind power to make electric energy rather than fossil fuels?

Idea to Examples

- Work with a group of classmates to list all the ways that electric energy is used in your classroom. Compare your group's responses to those of another group.
- Give examples of the various energy sources that are used to make electric energy.

Examples to Idea

- What did the energy from the bodies of plants and animals from ancient times become in modern times? How does this relate to electricity?
- Light, heat, and motion are examples of what?

Evaluation

- Who do you think contributed most to making the electricity we enjoy today possible? Why did you choose that person?

Journal

A journal is usually a written collection of reflections. However, journals can also include drawings, songs, and other entries.

Journaling is one way for students to self-assess, giving them opportunities to integrate, synthesize, evaluate, and reflect on learning. Here are some ideas of what students can do in their journals.

- Mind Map (see Getting Ready, page 61)
- List questions they have about electricity. How can they find answers? What do they observe? What experiments can they do? What research resources will they use?
- Record what they learn as in a science log. What do they understand that they didn't before? Which aspects of electricity do they feel they understand? What have they learned about themselves as learners?
- Establish connections between this study and other science studies or other subjects they have studied.
- Note aspects of electricity they don't understand and their next steps for learning.

Portfolio Possibilities

A portfolio is a collection of student work that provides evidence of growth of knowledge, skills, and attitudes. Portfolios provide a systematic and organized way for students and teachers to collect and review evidence of student learning over time. A key component of portfolios is a reflection page to go with each entry and with the portfolio as a whole. For more information on portfolios, see page xii. Ask students to include any or all of the following in their electricity portfolios:

- First drawings of open and closed circuits
- List of materials that conduct and do not conduct electricity
- Picture of the process of making electric energy
- Test questions from the "Electric Connection Rap"
- Pictures and written descriptions of any gadgets the student made

---

Materials for Electric Study

- ▶ a self-closing plastic bag (such as ZipLock)
- ▶ a D-cell battery
- ▶ a flashlight bulb
- ▶ a plastic-coated wire with the plastic removed about 3 centimeters up on both ends
- ▶ additional batteries
- ▶ wire
- ▶ little motors
- ▶ buzzers
- ▶ rubber bands
- ▶ battery holders
- ▶ bulb holders
- ▶ scrap wood
- ▶ polystyrene

- ▶ aluminum foil
- ▶ coat hangers
- ▶ empty cans and other containers
- ▶ straws
- ▶ clay
- ▶ glue
- ▶ broken appliances
- ▶ thread spools
- ▶ cardboard tubes
- ▶ hammers
- ▶ nails
- ▶ screwdrivers
- ▶ pliers
- ▶ other tools

Discovering the Concepts

The activities guide students to discover the concepts. More about this phase and a constructivist approach to learning is on page xiv. This chart shows the steps for the Taxonomy for Discovery. These steps structure the unit for true discovery. A rubric for the taxonomy is on page 148.

Experiencing	**Organizing**	**Sharing**	**Processing**
Investigate. Make observations. Collect data.	Make charts, graphs. Look for patterns.	Compare observations with those of other groups.	What did we learn?

Laying a Foundation

During these activities, students discover for themselves how to make a closed circuit so a bulb lights. They also discover that metal is a good conductor of electricity. These discoveries form the foundation for further investigations into electricity.

Batteries and Bulbs: Discover Ways to Make the Bulb Light

Objectives

- Students discover several ways to make circuits using batteries, bulbs, and wires.
- Students hone their inquiry skills as they work their way through Cohen's Taxonomy for Discovery.

Materials

▶ D-cell batteries

▶ flashlight bulbs

▶ plastic-coated wire cut into pieces 20 to 30 centimeters long with the plastic stripped off the ends about 3 centimeters

▶ ZipLock plastic sandwich bags or other plastic bags with zippered closings

Procedure

Step 1. Put a battery, bulb, and wire into each plastic bag. Pass out one bag to each student.

Step 2. Guide students through the stages of the Taxonomy for Discovery.

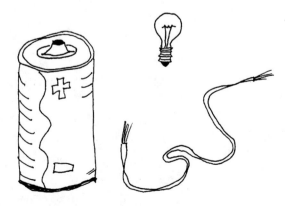

Experiencing: Ask students to find more than one way to light the bulb. If some students have been through this exercise before, ask them to hold off for a while before lighting the bulb to give other students a chance to try some different ways themselves. Struggling with the problem for a while will deepen students' motivation to get and understand an answer. Eventually a few students will create a circuit and light the bulb. Other students will imitate them, which is natural.

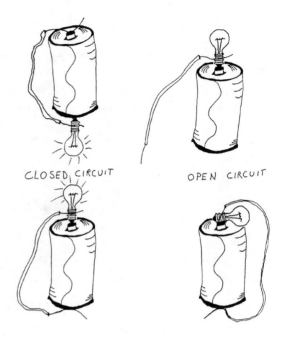

CLOSED CIRCUIT   OPEN CIRCUIT

Organizing: Students make a chart that shows three ways to make the bulb light, and three ways that fail to make the bulb light. Then students write paragraphs that describe what the ways that make the bulb light have in common, and what the ways that don't make the bulb light have in common.

Sharing: Students share their ideas about what is necessary to make a bulb light. Any disagreements can be resolved by experimenting more.

Processing: The class discussion helps students integrate their findings. Introduce important vocabulary. Students probably already knew that a battery causes electric current. They probably also knew that a bulb needs electric current. What they may not have realized is that both the side of the base of the light bulb and the bottom of the light bulb must be touched as do the two terminals of the battery. The following information should be included:

- For the bulb to light, the battery's two terminals must contact wire or the metal base of the bulb. The bottom of the bulb and side of the base need to be touched. A closed circuit is a complete path of electric current. The bulb lights. An open circuit has a break in the electric current. The bulb does not light.

- Students write any revisions of their ideas that have come from the previous discussion. They test any new hypotheses.

- Once students understand the concept of open and closed circuits, learning about good conductors and poor conductors is a simple, logical next step.

Good Conductors, Poor Conductors, and Insulators

Objectives
- Students discover that objects made of metal complete a circuit, enabling the bulb to light.
- Students discover that objects made of materials such as wood, plastic, rubber, and paper do not complete a circuit, so the bulb does not light.
- Students are able to use the terms *good conductors, poor conductors,* and *insulators.*
- Students continue to hone their inquiry skills as they work their way through the Taxonomy for Discovery.

Materials

► batteries, bulbs, and wire from the previous activity

► objects of various materials around the classroom or that students have

Procedure

Step 1. Place a key or an earring on top of the battery and ask students what they think will happen if you put the bulb attached to the wire on top of the key or earring. When students see that the bulb lights, they are highly motivated to find other materials that complete the circuit.

Step 2. Once students have the idea, they can use various materials in the room to go through Cohen's Taxonomy of Discovery.

Experiencing: Students use personal belongings and objects around the room to find materials that they think will close the circuit and make the bulb light. Students note their findings.

Organizing: Students make a chart that shows materials that close the circuit and those that don't.

Sharing: Students compare charts.

Processing: Students discuss and reflect to reinforce concepts and introduce vocabulary. It shouldn't take them long to discern a pattern. Objects made of metal close the circuit. Metals are *good conductors* of electric charge. Good conductors have electric charges that are loosely bound so that they can move easily. Objects that don't complete the circuit are *poor conductors* or *nonconductors*. Objects that don't let their charges move, such as plastic and rubber, are *insulators*. Insulators are very strong nonconductors; they have electric charges that are tightly bound. The metal inside wire makes a good path for electric current. The plastic or rubber that covers the metal keeps people from getting shocked. When students understand how conductors work, they are ready to use bulb holders, battery holders, switches, and all the other paraphernalia that go with making electrical gadgets.

Constructing the Learning

This section presents ways to make circuit parts from readily available materials. See page 67. Students make series and parallel circuits and electromagnets They add to their knowledge by making some electrical gadgets. Finally, students discover how electricity is generated in the power plant and carried to their homes.

Series and Parallel Circuits

Once students understand the concept of metal as a conductor of electric charge, they can use battery and bulb holders to make series and parallel circuits and compare their properties.

This activity takes students through Cohen's Taxonomy for Discovery as they follow the current through the circuit, and as test their hypotheses about whether, if they unscrew one bulb in a circuit, the remaining bulb will stay on.

Materials (For each group of students)

► D-cell battery

► battery holder

► 2 bulb holders

► 4 wires, each about 10 cm long

► 2 flashlight bulbs

Procedure

Step 1. Students make a series circuit with one battery and battery holder, two bulbs and bulb holders, and three wires. Students hook up the battery, three wires and two bulbs as in the diagram.

SERIES CIRCUIT

PARALLEL CIRCUIT

Step 2. Students make a parallel circuit with one battery and battery holder, two bulbs and bulb holders, and four wires. Students hook up the battery, four wires and two bulbs as in the diagram.

Experiencing: Students make the series and parallel circuits and follow the course of the electric current through the circuit with each set up. They write down their ideas of the sequence of the flow.

Organizing: Students clarify the sequence of the electric flow in the above activity. For example, in the series circuit, the electrical energy flows from the battery to the wire to the first bulb, to the wire, to the second bulb, to the wire to the battery. With the parallel circuit, however, the electrical energy travels from the battery to the wire to one bulb, then to a wire and back. For the second bulb, the electrical energy travels from the battery to the first wire to the second wire then to the light bulb. Then the energy flows to the third and fourth wire and back to the battery.

Sharing: Groups share their ideas about how the electrical energy flows through each circuit with other groups.

Processing: As a result of the class discussion about their observations, students make predictions about what would happen to the second bulb if they were to unscrew one bulb in the series circuit and why. They also make predictions about the second bulb in the parallel circuit. At this point they can test out their predictions by unscrewing one bulb in each circuit and seeing what happens. Students understand that in the series circuit, the second bulb needs the first bulb to close the circuit. In the parallel circuit, the two bulbs are independent of each other.

These understandings will help students when they make circuits for their gadgets and when they study what makes the lights go on in their homes.

Circuit Parts

If your school doesn't have electricity kits, there are some easy ways for students to put together parts for the circuits they will be making in this study:

Bulb Holders

Bulb holders hold bulbs in such a way that two wires can touch the bulb in places that will cause it to light.

- Stick a bulb in a piece of clay. Insert the wires in the clay with one touching the bottom and another touching the side of the metal part of the bulb.
- Stick a bulb in a piece of folded cardboard with one bare wire wrapped around the middle of the metal part of the bulb and another touching the bottom of the bulb.
- Put two brass brads in a box or on a piece of cardboard. Connect each brad to a wire underneath. Connect a paper clip to one brass brad, and open the clip to hold the bulb on top of the other brass brad.

Battery Holders

Use rubber bands or tape to hold wires to the ends of the battery.

Wire

Wire can be bare or covered with plastic, cloth, or enamel. Students will need to peel or scrape the ends of covered wire to make connections. Wire can be made from aluminum foil. Sometimes the telephone company will give you free wire.

Switches

Switches are important. They are a way for students to make sure their gadgets aren't left on when they don't want them to be. Following are some easy-to-make switches.

- Students get a small box, two brass brads, wire, and a paper clip. They push the brads into the top of the box, then wrap the wire around the bottom of the two brads. They connect the paper clip to the top of one brass brad. When the paper clip touches the other brad, the circuit is closed. When it doesn't touch the other brad, the circuit is open and the gadget turns off.
- Get a spring clothespin. Use the clothespin to clamp the wires together for a closed circuit. Open the clothespin to open the circuit.
- Insert the two wires into a ball of clay so they are touching. Pull out one wire to open the circuit.

Circuit Problems

If students' gadgets won't work, ask them to check the following things:

- Is the battery dead?
- If the gadget requires more than one battery, are the wrong terminals connected?
- Is there insufficient power (too few batteries)?
- Is the light bulb burnt out or loose?
- Are some wires loose?
- Are the wires separated by paint, rust, or is tape in the way?
- Are some wires or other metal touching that shouldn't be?
- Is there an open switch that should be closed?

Electromagnets

Building electromagnets can help students make sense of motors.

Materials

- ▶ D-cell battery
- ▶ 2 meters of thin, plastic-coated wire for each student or pair of students
- ▶ iron nail
- ▶ straight pins

Procedure

Step 1. To demonstrate an electromagnet to the students, wrap two meters of thin, plastic-coated wire as tightly as possible around an iron nail.

Step 2. Attach the ends of the wire to a D-cell battery with a lot of juice.

Step 3. Ask students to count how many straight pins the magnet can pick up.

Experiencing: Students experiment with wrapping different amounts of wire around the nail and comparing the number of pins the electromagnet can pick up.

Organizing: Students organize the results.

Sharing: Students share their findings with others.

Processing: In the class discussion, the following information about how electromagnets relate to motors should be included:

- The word *motor* comes from a word meaning *to move.*
- A motor has an electromagnet.
- Alternating current changes the direction of the electromagnet's North and South Poles. Another magnet, the rotor magnet, is attached to the rotor, the part of the motor that turns. The electromagnet's North Pole pulls on the rotor magnet's South Pole. Then, the current in the electromagnet switches directions. The electromagnet's North Pole becomes a South Pole, which pushes away the South Pole of the rotor magnet. The rotor turns which allows the appliance to move and do work.

Making Gadgets

Making gadgets allows students to use the information they have learned about electric currents in an enjoyable way. There are a number of possible methods to make these gadgets. Students don't need to follow the directions exactly as long as they remember the basic principles of a closed circuit. The directions might even give them ideas for making a very different gadget of their own invention.

Objective

- Students deepen their understanding of electrical circuits, conductors, ways electrical appliances work, and the skills involved in scientific inquiry.

Materials

▶ See individual activities.

Procedure

Step 1. Follow the procedures listed under the individual gadgets. Students may also find gadgets in other books or come up with their own inventions.

Step 2. As students work on their gadgets, they will go through the stages of the Taxonomy for Discovery.

Experiencing: Students make the gadgets.

Organizing: Students organize their problems and findings in written form.

Sharing: Students confer with one another about their challenges and discoveries in making the gadgets. They allow other students to try out their gadgets.

Processing: The class discusses their experiences. They synthesize their findings. They demonstrate their gadgets to compare the circuits.

Circuit Challenger: Make Your Own Teaching Machine!

A circuit challenger is a teaching machine that helps students review material in any subject. They can make big circuit challengers to cover a bulletin board, or small ones the size of regular paper. The following instructions are for a simple circuit challenger. Once students have made it, they can change the questions and answers easily to practice new material. They can also use wires and brass brads with cardboard or wooden bases instead of the foil suggested.

Materials

▶ aluminum foil
▶ masking or cellophane CD
▶ tag board or cardboard
▶ paper
▶ circuit tester: battery, wire, and bulb, or a continuity tester from a hardware store

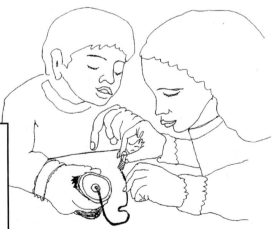

Continuity Tester

A continuity tester is an inexpensive instrument that contains a bulb, a small battery, and a piece of wire. The continuity tester is easier to handle because it is one piece.

Procedure

Step 1. Students make up some questions and answers for any subject—science, music, art, social studies, math, basketball. They might choose to write out definitions or draw pictures of terms. For example, they might draw the parts of a flower and ask the player to match the labels to the correct flower parts.

Step 2. They place a piece of paper on the tag board or cardboard and punch holes where they want the questions and answers.

Step 3. Students put some strips of CD on the dull side of the aluminum foil to make foil strips. Make sure the pieces of CD don't touch each other.

Step 4. They cut out the foil strips along the edges of the CD, cutting out one foil strip for each pair of questions and answers. Each strip needs to be the correct length to cover the holes next to the corresponding question and answer.

Step 5. On the back of the tag board, students CD each strip so that the foil side can be seen through the holes on the front of the tag board. The foil strips must connect the hole next to the question with the hole next to the answer. No foil should be visible on the back of the tag board. Even a tiny bit of foil visible on the edge of the strips could complete a circuit and make the bulb light for the wrong answer.

Step 6. On the front of the paper, students write their questions and answers, making sure the placement matches the foil pathways.

Step 7. Students test the circuit challenger by hooking up the bulb, wire, and battery, or the continuity tester so that they can make a closed circuit when the ends of the wire touch the foil in the matching holes. When they touch the wires to the question and its matching answer, the bulb will light.

Step 8. Students cover the back of the circuit challenger so their friends can't see the answers.

Step 9. They label the back and keep a file of the configurations so they can use the same board with new questions and subjects whenever they want. The board can be turned for a different configuration.

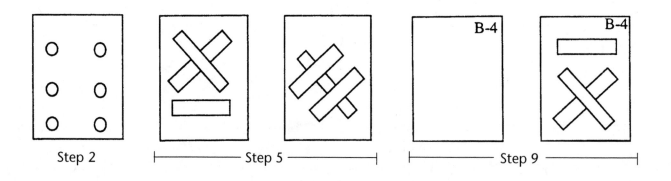

Step 2   ├──────── Step 5 ────────┤   ├──────── Step 9 ────────┤

Nerve Tester

Students can use this gadget to test hand steadiness. They will move a playing stick along a curvy wire. As long as their hands are steady, the circuit will stay open and the bulb won't light. When their hands shake, the playing stick will touch the wire, the circuit will close, and the bulb will light! They can see how far they can go before the bulb lights up. It can be even more fun to hook the nerve tester up to a buzzer rather than a light bulb.

Materials

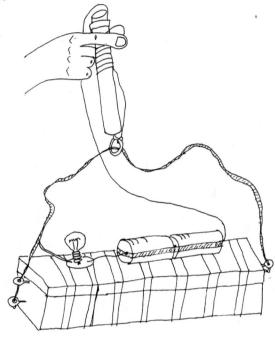

- ▶ wire coat hanger
- ▶ sandpaper
- ▶ shoe box or other similar-sized box
- ▶ D-cell battery
- ▶ battery holder
- ▶ wire
- ▶ bulb and bulb holder or buzzer
- ▶ paper or paint to cover the box
- ▶ colored CD
- ▶ screw eyes

Procedure

Step 1. Students paint the box or cover it with paper. They divide the box into sections, mark the sections with colored CD.

Step 2. A pencil makes a good playing stick. Students take a long piece of bare wire and run it along the pencil. At one end of the pencil, they make a loop with the bare wire about as big around as their finger. They wrap masking CD around the part of the wire and pencil they will hold.

Step 3. If the coat hanger has a coating on it, students will need to sand it off with sandpaper. Otherwise, the coating will insulate the wire, and they won't be able to get a closed circuit. With pliers, they bend and curve the coat hanger.

Step 4. Students twist two small screw eyes along each end of the box, one near the top and the other near the bottom. They put the ends of the coat hanger into the screw eyes to hold it in place.

Step 5. Students place the bulb holder or buzzer on the box. They wire it and push the wires through the box, connecting one wire to one end of the battery and the other to the coat hanger.

Step 6. Students connect the wire on the playing stick to the other terminal of the battery.

Step 7. Now they can test their nerve!! They can do experiments to see who has the steadiest hands: boys or girls, grown-ups or young people. They record their results.

Lights for a Doll House
Materials
- doll house or boxes to make rooms for a doll house
- light bulbs for each room
- wire (lots of it)
- batteries
- switches
- clay
- sticks
- thread spools
- corks

Procedure
Step 1.   Students connect light bulbs to the walls or ceiling of the dollhouse. They can also make standing lamps or table lamps with clay, sticks, cork, or other materials they find.

Step 2.   Using what they already know about circuits, students wire the doll house and connect the wires to batteries. The batteries could be outside of the doll house. The batteries are the power source. In the processing phase, ask them what the source of power for lights is in their homes.

Alarms
Materials
- buzzer
- spring clothespin
- metal thumbtacks
- wire
- cardboard
- wax
- string

Procedure
Step 1.   Students wrap wire around two metal thumbtacks and insert them into the inside of the jaws of the clothespin so their heads touch.

Step 2.   They attach the wires to a buzzer and battery to make a closed circuit.

Step 3.   They can add a switch so they can turn it off when they're not using it.

Step 4.   They can make a burglar alarm by putting a piece of cardboard attached to a string between the tacks in the jaws of the clothespin. Attach the clothespin to one part of the door, and the string to another part so it is taut. If someone trips over the string or opens the door, the string will pull out, the circuit (thumbtacks) will close, and the alarm will sound.

Step 5.   They can also make a water alarm by putting an aspirin or sugar cube between the tacks in the clothespin and placing the whole contraption in water. When the aspirin or sugar cube dissolves, the circuit will close, and the alarm will sound.

Step 6.   Finally, students make a fire alarm by putting a ball of wax between the tacks in the clothespin. If a fire were to start, the heat would melt the wax, and the circuit would close.

How Power Plants Create Electrical Currents

Objectives

- Students understand how to follow the production of electric power in a power plant.
- Students are able follow the circuit made by electric current from the power plant to our homes and back to the power plant.
- Students understand the relationship between the electric current that comes from the generator to wall outlets, and the current that comes from batteries to bulbs.

Materials

- hot plate or stove top
- tea kettle
- fan blade template
- cardboard
- pencils
- pins
- CD
- magnet

Procedure

Step 1. Introduce the activity by telling students that a power plant is where electricity is made. They are going to make a model of a power plant, guessing how each part of the model corresponds to a part in a real power plant.

Step 2. Guide students through the steps of the Taxonomy for Discovery.

Experiencing: Students make a model of a power plant by following these directions.

Step 1. They cut out fan blades from cardboard using a template.

Step 2. Students attach the fan blades to the eraser of the pencil with a pin.

Step 3. They CD a magnet to the lead end of the pencil.

Step 4. Students coil about one meter of copper wire around the magnet.

Step 5. They boil some water in a teakettle to make steam without getting close to the steam; it can burn. The purpose is for them to see that steam can move things.

Step 6. Students turn the fan blades above the steam, pretending that the steam is turning the blades. Steam makes pressure that can do work. The fan blades turn the pencil with the magnet on the end.

Step 7. Students attach the ends of the wire wrapped around the magnet to a meter or compass. As the magnet moves, the needle in the meter or compass will move. This shows the wire has current.

Students write down their observations and inferences or guesses about how the elements of the model relate to a real power plant.

Organizing: Students organize their observations into a sequence, then note the causes and effects in the sequence; for example, "The steam makes the fan blades turn. The blades turn the magnet. The magnet creates a current in the coil of wire that surrounds it." They also include their guesses about how each element of the model relates to a real power plant.

Sharing: In small groups, students share their observations, sequences, and guesses about the relationship of the model to real power plants.

Processing: For the class discussion, photocopy the picture of a power plant (page 55). Either make one for each student or enlarge the picture so the class can see it. Students might make the following connections between the actual power plant and their model:

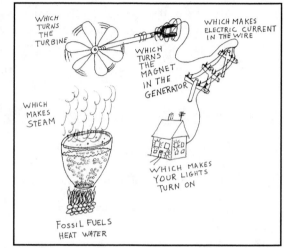

- The fan blades correlate to the turbine in the power plant. *Turbine* comes from a word that means "whirl" or "spin."

- The pencil corresponds to the shaft. In the power plant, the shaft is connected to a big magnet surrounded by wire in the generator. As the magnet turns, electric current is generated.

- The magnet and wire represent the generator in the power plant.

- The steam from the teakettle correlates to the steam most power plants make to turn the turbine. They burn coal, oil, or natural gas. Nuclear power plants use a nuclear reaction to heat the water into steam. Some plants use solar power to heat the water. Hydroelectric plants don't make steam at all; they use the energy created by the falling water to turn the turbine.

Electric currents are created in the generator. The generator contains a giant magnet and coil of wire. As the turbine turns, the shaft turns. As the shaft turns, the magnet within the coil of wire turns. As the magnet turns, electric charges begin to move within the wire.

The electric current travels along the wire and out of the power plant at 24,000 volts to a transformer. Transformers change current from low to high or from high to low voltage. The transformer raises voltage to 345,000 volts to travel long distances through high-voltage wire. Other transformers lower the voltage to 13,800 volts for factories and large businesses, or to 110 or 220 volts for homes. The story on page 78 reinforces this discovery activity.

Students might also consider ways the information they have learned about circuits using batteries and bulbs relates to electrical energy in their homes:

- The power source they used with the flashlight bulb was a battery. The power source for the electric current in their homes is a power plant.

- Electric wires in utility poles carry the electric current between the power plant and their homes just as wires connected to a battery carry electric current to the flashlight bulb.

- A break in the circuit to or from the power plant causes a blackout in a city, just as a break in the battery and bulb circuit keeps the bulb from lighting.

- Plugs and outlets each have two prongs, one for the wires that are bringing the electric charge to the light or appliance, another to take the electric charge from the light or appliance back to the power plant. In the same way, a light bulb has two wires connected to the battery's two terminals. The "Electric Connection Rap" on page 84 and the CD reinforces how electricity gets to their homes.

Creating a Context for the Discoveries

BEN FRANKLIN

Play: History of Electricity

The play gives a big picture overview of the subject matter, including relevant issues and important vocabulary and concepts without a lecture. Page xx has more information about plays. This play is on the CD.

Cast: Michelle, Narrator, Benjamin Franklin, Thales, Luigi Galvani, Alessandro Volta, Michael Faraday, Thomas Edison

Michelle: Hi. My name is Michelle.

Oh, great. I have to do this dumb presentation about electricity at school tomorrow, and I don't know anything about it. Who cares about electricity anyway? (Sounds of thunder)

Hey, why did all the lights go out? What happened to the TV? And the CD player? Better get a candle. Where is that candle we had in the pumpkin last Halloween? Guess this will do. (Match lights.) Hmmm, a situation as bad as this calls for a snack. What? Even the refrigerator isn't working! (knock, knock, knock) Someone's at the door. Why didn't they ring the doorbell? Guess that isn't working either. (eeerrrrkkkk—Door creeks open.)

What? It must be Halloween! You look just like that guy on the hundred dollar bill! Who is that guy, Ben Franklin?

Narrator: Enter Benjamin Franklin holding a kite with a key on the end of its string.

Ben Franklin: My dear young friend, did I hear you say that you don't care about electricity? Statements like that make me roll over in my grave! That's why I'm here. Permit me to come in. I have a few things to say. First, "to appreciate electricity, one has to know its history."

Michelle: Wait a minute! Who are you?

Ben Franklin: You were right the first time. I am Ben Franklin.

Michelle: So you are one of our country's founding fathers. Well, why are you carrying that kite? What's that got to do with founding our country?

Ben Franklin: Actually, my dear friend, I was a man with many interests, one of the greatest of which was electricity. Of course, this was years before there were lights, TVs, and power plants. I used this kite to prove that lightning is a form of electricity.

Michelle: How did you do that?

Ben Franklin: When my little daughter Sally had held a knitting needle right next to one of my electricity experiments, sparks flew out of it! That gave me the idea of putting a metal rod in the end of a kite, attaching the kite to a string, and putting a key on the end of the string to let the electric fire out. On that day in 1752, I proved what I believed. Lightning *is* electricity.*

Michelle: I guess that was a big chance you were taking. If the lightning had killed you, you never would have signed the Declaration of Independence.

---

* Although it is part of the legend, if Franklin had held onto the kite while it was struck, he would have been killed. Be sure students know not to try this experiment at home.

Science for Every Learner, © 2000 Zephyr Press, Tucson, Arizona

Ben Franklin: Quite so, quite so, my young friend. Anyone experimenting with electricity must take safety precautions.

Michelle: Say, you must have been the first person to ever think about electricity, huh?

Ben Franklin: On the contrary, my dear friend, let me introduce you to someone who was considered to be the first philosopher to appear in ancient Greece. Philosophy, you may know, is the study of knowledge.

Narrator: Enter Thales.

Michelle: Whoa, who is this guy in the white sheet?

Thales: Good evening, Michelle. My name is Thales. I was working with electricity 2,500 years ago. I found that if I rubbed a yellow stone called amber with fur, the stone could pick up feathers and other light materials. My experiments were examples of static electricity. The word for amber in Greek was *electron*. So my experiments gave electricity its name.

Michelle: So, Mr. Thales, the Greeks must have been the first people to work with electricity, right?

Thales: Actually, Michelle, the Chinese were using magnetism 500 years before my time. As you continue your studies, you will find that electricity and magnetism work hand in hand. Now, my experiments were only with static electricity. The ability to harness current, or moving electricity, has made possible the lights, TV, and all the conveniences to which you are accustomed. Please meet my friends from Italy, some key players in this advance.

Narrator: Enter Luigi Galvani.

Galvani: Buona notte, signores. Hello, Michelle. So strange, so strange. I was studying a dissected frog in my laboratory. When I put a copper hook on the frog's leg, then touched the leg with iron, the leg would jump. It danced—even though the frog was dead! It's true, I swear! I was sure the electricity was in the muscles or nerves of animals.

Narrator: Enter Alessandro Volta.

Volta: I, however, discovered the true reason why that frog's leg danced. It was not animal electricity. It was chemical! The two metals, copper and iron, in the liquid of the frog's body had a chemical reaction! I used this insight to make the first electric battery!

Galvani: (resentfully) I think the first battery was a frog.

Volta: Don't be silly, Signore Galvani. In 1796, I discovered that chemical energy could create electrical energy! Batteries you use today are based on this same principle! Stick a copper and zinc nail next to each other in a lemon, then touch the nails with your tongue. You will feel a tingle. The tingle is the electric current in the flow of your lemon battery!!

Galvani: (weeping) So, I was wrong. Boo hoo.

Ben Franklin: That is the nature of science, Signore Galvani. New discoveries may disprove prior theories, but your work made Signore Volta's work possible. Each succeeding generation of scientific researchers stands on the shoulders of those who came before them. In fact, Michelle, you and others of your generation may make scientific discoveries that make scientific ideas that everyone believes true today obsolete.

Volta: Very true, Signore Franklin. On the shoulders, si. From here on, Michelle, notice that we are discussing current electricity. Current electricity always starts with a power source. The electric current goes through wires from the power source and back to the power source in a circle. If there is a break in the circle of wire, you have no circuit. No circuit, no current electricity. Simple, eh?

Thales: Remember how I said that electricity and magnetism worked together? Here comes the person who used that knowledge to discover ways to harness electricity that changed the world forever!

Narrator: Enter Michael Faraday.

Michael Faraday: A bit of my story may be relevant. I was born to a poor family outside of London, quit school at thirteen, and worked in a bookbinding shop. I happened to enjoy reading the books I bound. My favorites were the books about electricity. I wanted in the worst way to become a philosopher. (In the 1800s scientists were called philosophers.) And I jolly well succeeded. Read about my life sometime to find out how a poor bloke like me became a respected researcher at the Royal Institution. My experiments there on the relationship between magnetism and electricity made it possible for me to invent the first electric motor and the first electric generator.

Michelle: Sweet! So, how did you do that?

Michael Faraday: In 1821 I hooked up a battery...

Volta: Thanks to me, Volta!

Faraday: (disconcerted) Yes, quite. When I hooked up a battery to a magnet, a wire moved around and around the magnet. I turned electrical energy into mechanical energy!

Michelle: So does that mean that everything with a motor in it has a magnet in it? The CD player, the electric mixer, the hair dryer, the fan, the vacuum cleaner...?

Michael Faraday: Quite so. In fact, if you walked around with a magnet, you would find it attracted to the magnets in the appliances all over your house.

So, on with my story. Ten years later, I found another use for magnetism and electricity. I discovered that if you turn a magnet around and around inside a coil of wire, you create electricity. The mechanical energy required to turn the magnet transforms magnetic energy into electrical energy.

Ben Franklin: Yes, today, power plants all over the world use Faraday's discovery to generate electric current. This discovery is the foundation of the world as you know it.

Michael Faraday: (modestly) Oh, please, Mr. Franklin.

Ben Franklin: Here comes my admirable friend, Thomas Edison.

Thomas Edison: Yes. Hello, Michelle. I built on the discoveries of my distinguished colleagues here. Because of my invention, electric lights began to light up cities and towns everywhere.

Ben Franklin: You lived to see the world changed because of your inventions. By the time your life ended in 1939, almost everyone was enjoying the electric lights and the phonograph that you invented.

Thales: Of course, all these benefits depend on electricity. The knowledge the world has about electricity is based on an accumulation of research over thousands of years.

Thomas Edison: Just so, Thales. And people are taking our discoveries further. Today, tiny electrical circuits in computers are making possible a revolution in the way people work, play, and communicate with each other! Researchers today and in the future are finding improved sources of energy to make electricity that are kinder to the planet than the fossil fuels you have been using. Solar energy, wind energy, fusion. The possibilities are exciting!

Michelle: I see. Each person played a part in making this great thing available to all of us! Hey, look! The lights just came back on! Yeeaa!!

Ben Franklin: That may be because you have come to your senses and recognize the value of electricity!

Volta: Or perhaps it is because the electric company just fixed a power line.

Ben Franklin: Er, yes, well, the point is that the human race's relationship to electricity has a great history, and great things are yet to come!

All: (eerie echo voices) Good-bye, Michelle. Until we meet again.

Narrator: (eeerrrrkkkk—Door creaks shut.)

Science for Every Learner, © 2000 Zephyr Press, Tucson, Arizona

Story: Energy Transfer—From the Sun to Electricity

You may tell stories with rich sensory descriptions and as if the students were actually in the story. Such techniques can help students develop their ability to make internal visual images, which is useful for mathematical thinking and problem solving in general. Stories provide another way to reinforce vocabulary and concepts. Page xx has more information about stories.

Close your eyes and pretend you have a special, new kind of job. You are an energy transfer watcher! Pretend you can move around in strange and astonishing ways with special eyes that see invisible energy. Now, feel yourself hurtling through time and space to watch the amazing transference of energy from one form to another.

It is millions of years ago. Watch the Sun shining its energy. Feel its heat and light. Smell the warm, moist Earth. It is quiet. Look, a green plant is bending toward the Sun. Watch the plant capture the Sun's light to make food! What's that noise? Boom. Boom. Boom. Listen to the heavy, plodding footsteps. Is it a dinosaur? See it eat the plant. Can you hear it chew? See the energy transfer to the animal. Uh, oh! The animal dies. Watch in fast motion as pressures from the Earth squeeze the animal's energy together with other plants and animals over millions of years into coal, oil or natural gas. These are fossil fuels, concentrated energy that leads back to the Sun!

Now time travel up to the present. Whoosh, watch the years spin by! Things have changed, haven't they? Look at those giant buildings and roads. Listen to all the noise! What's that, an oil well? Look, listen, and smell as the humans take the coal, oil or natural gas energy out of the ground and transport it to the power plant. Watch the fossil fuels burn. Can you smell them? See the heat released from that concentrated form of energy! Listen as the heat energy transfers to some water. Feel the water soak up more and more heat energy and turn from a liquid into steam. The steam is under high pressure. Watch out! It's hot!

Listen as the steam blasting out of a nozzle hits fans on the end of a shaft called *a turbine*.

Whrrrrr. The heat energy of the steam is moving the fans around and around and around. Don't get dizzy! This motion is called *mechanical energy*. The heat energy makes mechanical energy. Look at the magnet at the other end of the shaft. See the coil of wire surrounding the magnet. This is a generator. Watch! As the mechanical energy of the whirling fans in the turbine turns the magnet, electric charges begin to flow. This flow is called *electric current*. See, the mechanical energy of the whirling fans uses magnetic energy to make electric energy. Watch that electric energy transfer down the wire. Wheeeee!

Travel along the wires that carry the electric energy as they come out of the power plant. Travel above the ground from pole to pole. Now the wires are going underground into a city. Where are you now? You are in the wires going right into your own house!

Here comes an energy transfer! See the electric energy move through the wires in the wall of your house to a lamp that is plugged into the wall. See the wires go in a circle from the power plant to the lamp and back to the power plant again. A power line down anywhere on the route from the power plant to your home and back means there will be no electric current to your home. Here comes another energy transfer! Watch the electric energy transfer to the metal in the filament of the lamp. The electric energy is making heat and light energy.

Now, think back to the beginning. Where did that energy start? With the Sun, of course! The energy stored in fossil fuels comes from the Sun. Fly around the world now. (Yes, you can fly, too, when you pretend.) See the power plants using fossil fuels to make electric energy. Look, the fossil fuels are polluting the earth. When fossil fuels get used up, it will take millions of years to replace them.

Let's look around and find some more Earth-friendly ways to transfer the Sun's energy to make electricity. Here is a family that uses wind to power a little generator just for their home. Watch the Sun transfer its heat to the Earth. Some parts of the Earth are heating up more than others. This makes air move. Moving air is wind. Watch the wind blowing around the planet. Listen to its roar! Watch the wind energy turn a magnet inside the family's little generator to create an electric current. Watch the little generator transfer wind energy into electric energy.

Look, a small town is harnessing the Sun's energy in solar collector mirrors tilted toward a water tank in a tower to make steam to turn the turbines. And here is a family using solar batteries to transfer the Sun's energy to electric energy directly, without turbines and generators. (This energy transfer is used frequently in the space program.) Fusion is an atomic reaction that happens inside the Sun. Scientists are working to develop fusion generators to make electric power safe and inexpensive in the future.

Travel ahead in time, oh energy transfer watcher! Do you see the world using safe, clean energy sources to make electric power?

Now slowly bring yourself back to the classroom and find yourself sitting comfortably in your desk, ready to talk about your journey.

Deepening the Learning

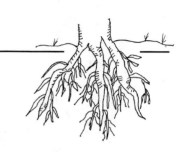

Multiple Intelligence Activities

Use a multiple intelligence approach to give students opportunities to develop more links in the brain for deeper understanding and greater emotional ties to the new learning. As students develop real-world connections and practice applying the new knowledge in a variety of circumstances, they enhance their ability to transfer their learning to new situations.

Verbal-Linguistic

- Students explain to someone else how electric energy is made.

- Students research microchips and how they work. A microchip contains tiny electric circuits in a microprocessor. Microchips are an innovation that make possible the personal computers, calculators, electronic games, digital watches, light-up sneakers, and many other things students enjoy.

- Students research superconductors. While the good conductors students found with the batteries and bulbs let electric charge move through, there is still some resistance; they lose some electric power. In 1986 scientists discovered a type of ceramic that could be cooled enough to allow it to become a superconductor. Superconductors do not resist the flow of electric charges. They make very powerful electromagnets.

Bodily-Kinesthetic

- Students follow Thales' suggestion for making a lemon battery in "The History of Electricity." They get a juicy lemon and stick one copper wire and one zinc wire into the lemon close together. When they touch the wires with their tongue, the tingle is the current created by their lemon battery.

- Students use the information on superconductors to build models of "Maglevs," magnetic levitation trains. These high-speed trains zoom along on a cushion of magnetism above a track. Students can build a model of a Maglev train. Bill Beaty's Web site at www.eskimo.com/~billb/ gives directions. He has other suggestions for science projects there, too.

- Students take apart old appliances that no one wants, with the cords removed. They try to figure out how the appliances work. Electric appliances that make heat probably have a heating element inside. Heating elements are like filaments in a light bulb in that they make heat and light.

- Take a class trip to your local power plant. Students see for themselves how the electric energy they use every day is made.

Logical-Mathematical

- Students read an electric meter and calculate the amount of money their family is spending on electricity each month. Electric companies use meters to tell how many kilowatt-hours of electricity people use each month. A kilowatt-hour (kwh) means 1,000 watts per hour. A watt is a unit of electric power. Students can practice with the following diagram first.

MULTIPLY BY TEN

KILOWATT-HOURS

Notice there are four dials. Students read the meter from the left. When arrows are between two numbers, they should use the lower number. The reading for this meter is 48040.

MULTIPLY BY TEN

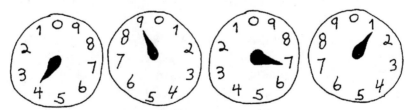

KILOWATT-HOURS

Suppose next month the meter looks like this: What is the reading for this meter? Students read the meters at their homes. If the cost of electric power is $.08 per kilowatt-hour, what is their family's electric bill for that month?

- Students group the appliances listed below into either necessities or luxuries.

air conditioner (one-room unit) 1,100 watts	fluorescent lights 15–40 watts
blender 300 watts	garbage disposal 450 watts
toaster 1,100 watts	hair dryer 1,250 watts
washing machine 700 watts	hot plate 1,500 watts
coffee maker 750 watts	lamps 60–150 watts
humidifier 350 watts	oil burner 250 watts
dishwasher 1,500 watts	portable fan 100 watts
iron 1,000 watts	radio 10 watts
electric blanket 200 watts	electric stove 3,500 watts
electric clock 2.5 watts	refrigerator 450 watts
clothes dryer 4,500 watts	sewing machine 75 watts
electric frying pan 1,200 watts	stereo 300 watts
electric water heater 4,500 watts	TV 200 watts
freezer 440 watts	vacuum cleaner 600 watts

- Using the same list as in the last activity, students pretend it is a hot summer day and they must clean a house. They calculate how long the chores would take them, and figure out which appliances they would need to use. Then they have a friend over to visit, and figure out which appliances they would use to entertain the friend. They calculate the cost of cleaning the house and entertaining their friend based on a cost of $.08 per kilowatt-hour; they graph the results.

Visual-Spatial

- Students make a mural that shows how electric energy is made and used.
- Students make a flow chart that shows each step of the process of harnessing and supplying electric energy.
- Students collect light bulbs. Bulbs can be incandescent or fluorescent. The first bulbs were incandescent. There were as many as 16 different-sized bases. In the early days, bulbs were often recycled. The filaments were replaced, and the air was sucked out so that there would be a vacuum. Some of the bulbs in the collection can be burned-out bulbs, in which the filaments have a break in the wire.

Interpersonal

- Students make a human circuit using an Energy Ball, a small white ball about the size of a ping pong ball that they can buy at a magic shop or novelty store. (An address where you can mail away for one is provided at the end of this study.) The Energy Ball contains a battery, an electric amplifier, and a light or a buzzer with two metal terminals on the surface. If one person touches the two terminals, the circuit will close, and the ball will light or the buzzer will buzz. A few people or the whole class can become part of the circuit. All but two people hold hands to form a circle. When the first person touches one terminal, and the last person touches the other terminal, the circuit will close and the Energy Ball will do its thing. How does this work? The battery inside the Energy Ball makes the charges in your skin start flowing. The electronic amplifier inside the energy ball amplifies this small current so that it becomes strong enough to light the bulb. If two people who are holding hands on the other side of the circle let go, the circuit will break and the Energy Ball will stop. It is important that the two people who are touching the terminals of the Energy Ball are not touching each other. Otherwise, those two will make their own little circuit, and the Energy Ball will keep working.

- Students interview a representative from the local electric company to find out the source of energy used to make the electricity that reaches their homes. Students get as many details as possible about how this company produces electric energy. They find out about the history of the company. Was electric energy made the same way when their grandparents were their age?

- Students get an e-mail (or regular mail) pen pal. They share how electric energy is made where they live and ask how it is made where the pen pal lives. How are the two processes similar and different?

Intrapersonal

- Students pretend to be light bulbs, utility poles, or electrical wires from a plant to a hospital and tell the story of their lives.

- Students imagine living in a world without electric power. They share what they would miss the most and why. How could they improve the quality of life?

Naturalist

- Students research an example of electricity that occurs in nature and share what they find with the class. They listen to other students' research and look for similarities between the examples.

Musical-Rhythmic

- Students listen to "The Electric Connection Rap" (page 84) on the CD for the rhythm and fun. They make up some dance steps to go with the rap and perform it with friends.

- Students also listen to "The Electric Connection Rap" for the information the rap imparts. They use the information to make up test questions about electricity for a partner. They use the rap to help answer the questions a partner makes for them.

The Electric Connection Rap

Ask students to follow the path an electric current takes from the power source (the generator) to their home. What are transformers and conductors? What is always necessary for the electric current to flow?

When we get wired we're a wild bunch
A-hoppin' and a-poppin' with lots of punch!
It doesn't take much, much to turn us on
It's fun to run when you're an electron!

We hook right up to our power source
And then we activate . . . with a lot of force!
We're hard to stop once we get goin'.
You know how it is when the juice is flowin' !

Transformers serve to slow us down
As we head from the generator for a night on the town.
In those wires, we zap right on through
Over ditches, highways, and your backyard, too!

Conductors they're called for those who don't know.
They're the stuff that really makes us go!
We only travel very first class—
Gold, silver, or copper, but never rubber or glass.

When we hit town, the place is ablaze.
We're wizards at finding our way through the maze!
When we find your toaster, we'll make that boy pop;
Let us into your oven, and watch that joker hop!

Refrain

It's electric; get connected!
We'll touch your phone and make it ring.
We'll warm your kettle and make it sing!
You name it. You want some flare?

Just flick that switch and WE ARE THERE!
We light right up when we make a connection.
And we've figured out the surest direction!
There's a secret behind our awesome power
Mysterious and beautiful as a little flower . . . .

Closing the circle is what it's all about
with not one piece missing or left out.
United we stand. Divided we fall.
It's as simple as that, now that we know it all!

Refrain

Words by Catherine Razi. Music by Shade Jenifer. Rappers: Shade Jenifer, Hugh Scott, and Gwen Jenifer.

Performance Task for the Electric Study

Performance tasks are products or performances you can use to assess student understanding. Understanding, in this sense, means the ability to apply facts, concepts, or skills to new situations. With performance tasks, the assessment is embedded in the product or performance itself.

Electric Day Celebration

Background

You have been working with electric energy, learning about its history, and working with electric circuits for some time now. With your class, you will now organize and put on an Electric Day Celebration to share the learning and the projects you have made.

Task

Make a gadget that requires an electric circuit to operate. Then, during an Electric Day Celebration, you will explain to students in other classes how your gadget works. You will also describe what makes the lights in your home and school go on.

Audience

The audience will be members of other classes who attend the Electric Day Celebration.

Procedure

Make gadgets or use ones you made during the study that use an electric circuit to light, heat, or move. Although any gadget you have made will do, try to create one that is different from those of classmates. The gadget should be safe and battery operated. Following are some suggestions.

your own invention	*a telegraph code sender and receiver*
a teaching machine	*a door bell*
a flashlight	*boats and a lighthouse*

Step 1. Choose an item from the list.

Step 2. Write down your plans, describing what your gadget will do when the circuit is closed.

Step 3. Make the gadget and a switch.

Step 4. Draw a picture that shows how a power plant makes electric energy for the lights in your house. Include the following:

the power plant	*generator*
the energy source your power plant uses	*transformers*
the turbine	*wires to your house*

Format adapted from "A Teacher's Guide to Performance-Based Learning and Assessment" (1996) and teachers of Connecticut's Pomraug School District 15.

Step 5. Use your picture to help you teach a visitor how lights go on. Compare the circuit that makes the lights go on in your home to the circuit that makes your gadget work. How are they similar? How are they different? For instance, what is the source of electrical energy for the circuit that lights your home? What is the source of energy for the circuit that works your gadget?

Rubric

A rubric provides criteria and standards for assessing a student's learning. A rubric also serves as a self-assessment tool for the students to use while designing the product or creating the performance. A rubric makes it possible for peers, teachers, and the students themselves to easily calculate a numerical score that represents the quality of the student's performance. **For more information about how to score the rubrics, please refer to number 5 on page xvi.**

Performance Rubric for the Electric Gadget

Criteria	Electric Expert	Currently Current	Needs a Jump Start
Gadget	Gadget is different from most others and it works.	Gadget is similar to others and works, or original and has some problems.	Gadget is incomplete, or if complete, it does not work.
The Circuit	Describes and demonstrates open and closed circuits.	Describes and demonstrates open and closed circuits.	Cannot describe or cannot demonstrate open and closed circuits.
Making Electric Energy: The Process	Picture and description are accurate and detailed.	Picture and description mostly accurate; some detail may be missing.	Picture and description missing or incomprehensible.

Some Places to Find Materials

▶ magic store for Energy Balls, or Safari, Ltd., Box 630685, Miami, FL 33163

▶ school electrical kit

▶ hardware stores

Extensions

Sometimes students' questions take them beyond their ability to observe and experiment directly. The World Wide Web and student trade books offer ideal opportunities for students and teachers to extend their research, often leading to new and better questions, observations, and experiments.

Web Addresses

www.eskimo.com/~billb/

Bill Beaty's site presents a wealth of information on teaching and learning about electric energy and electric circuits. It has background, theory, resources, and projects. Most importantly, it picks out a number of misconceptions about electricity—even those in science books and dictionaries—and sets the record straight.

www.can.cz/

This is the site of the Can Company in Czechoslovakia, which specializes in superconductors. The Can Company also puts out educational kits in English about superconductors.

www.learningteam.org

Has *Find it! Science: The Books You Need at Lightning Speed,* a CD-ROM with detailed descriptions of hundreds of science trade books.

www.fi.edu

Ask-an-expert service through Franklin Institute Science Museum allows you and your students to receive answers to your science questions from experts in the field.

Book Corner

Books related to the study can do much to spark student inquiry. In addition to science books, include biographies, fiction, poetry, dictionaries, encyclopedias, and other types. Create a center in the classroom with books, pictures, photographs, magazines, and CDs.

Almost any library has books with suggestions for electric gadgets and experiments that will interest and motivate your students to begin their own inquiries. The books listed below were helpful in designing this study. They all have interesting additional information and activities about electric energy.

Carroll, Kathleen. 1999. *Sing a Song of Science.* Tucson, Ariz.: Zephyr Press.

> Has rap, activities, and Web site addresses for information about energy sources; includes a CD with the rap.

Cole, Johanna. 1997. *The Magic School Bus and the Electric Field Trip.* New York: Scholastic Press.

A whimsical story in comic book format that includes a great deal of information about how electricity is generated and transported.

Gibson, Gary. 1995. *Science for Fun: Understanding Electricity.* Brookfield, Conn.: Copper Beech.

Includes good background information along with activities.

Parsons, Alexandra. 1997. *Make It Work! Electricity.* Chicago: World Book.

Has many hands-on activities.

The following biographies or others like them may be useful, too:

Adler, David. 1990. *Thomas Alva Edison: Great Inventor.* New York: Holiday House.

The story of a boy who didn't do well in school but went on to invent more than 1,093 different things, some of which changed the world.

Osborne, Mary Pope. 1989. *The Many Lives of Benjamin Franklin.* New York: Dial Books for Young Readers.

Includes Franklin's work with electricity, other inventions, and work as a diplomat, writer, printer, and abolitionist.

Glossary

An important part of science literacy is learning the language of science. Classrooms with posted words, stories, and games make vocabulary easy and fun.

closed circuit: a complete circle of conductors that allows the electric energy to flow through it

conductors: materials that allow electric charge to flow through

continuity tester: a device that contains a small battery, bulb, and metal ends that show whether or not a material can conduct electric charge; useful in building the Circuit Challenger or teaching machines

electric current: the flow of electrons

electric power: the transfer of electrical energy, measured in energy per second

electromagnet: a piece of iron or steel that is magnetized by the electric current in a coil of wire that surrounds it

electron: a tiny, negatively charged particle that comes from an atom

energy: the capacity to do work

fluorescent light bulb: a tube-shaped light bulb without a filament that gives off a cool light caused by a reaction of the gases inside it

fossil fuels: materials such as coal, oil, and natural gas that are formed from plants and animals that died millions of years ago and can be converted into energy

generator: a machine that converts mechanical energy to electrical energy; in a power plant, a generator contains a magnet that turns within a coil of wire.

incandescent light bulb: a bulb that gives off light due to a filament heating up and glowing when electric current passes through it

insulator: a material such as rubber, plastic, or glass that blocks the flow of electric charge

motor: a machine that converts electrical energy to mechanical energy. As electrical current keeps changing the poles of an electromagnet within the motor, another magnet, connected to a shaft, is forced to turn. The motor's turning shaft can be used for work.

open circuit: a circuit with a break that prevents the flow of electric charge

photovoltaic: providing a source of electric energy from light

solar energy: energy from the Sun; a clean source of electricity

superconductor: a material that allows the flow of electric charge without resistance

transformer: an electric device that can increase or decrease the voltage of electric current

turbine: a machine that has a shaft and rotor with blades that are turned by the force of steam, water, or other fluid

volt: a unit of measurement. A volt is like a "push" of electric current.

watt: a unit of electric power

wind energy: the motion of air caused by the Sun's uneven heating of the Earth's surface

Teacher Reflection

There is no need for teachers to know all the answers. One of the best things you can do for students is to serve as a model of a life-long learner. Use this reflection page to record some of your new understandings as you complete this unit.

What are some of your new understandings in regard to teaching and learning about this subject?

What in this unit worked for your students?

What were some problems that arose?

How could you overcome those problems next time?

What are some other things you would like to remind yourself about this study for next time?

Living Things Study

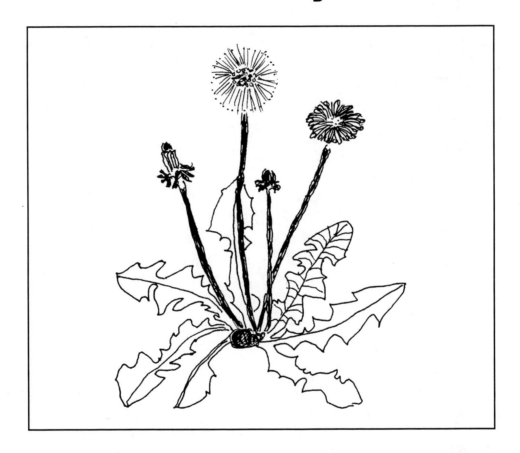

National Science Education Content Standards

As a result of the activities, all students should develop

- abilities necessary to do scientific inquiry   (standard A)
- understanding of the characteristics of organisms   (standard C)
- understanding of how organisms reproduce   (standard C)
- understanding of life cycles of organisms   (standard C)
- understanding of how organisms adapt   (standard C)
- understanding of how organisms interact with their environment   (standard C)

The Living Things Study at a Glance

Big Question

The essence of the study, through which all the objectives, activities and assessments are aligned:

- What does it mean to be alive?

Domain Matrix

A tool to check the alignment of objectives with activities and assessments (page 95).

Time Frame

From one quarter to a school year depending on your schedule and goals

Assessing Understanding

Portfolios and journals are ongoing projects. Think Trix questions assess student understanding and thinking skills along the way. The performance task with rubric culminates the study when students design a trail that demonstrates their understanding about living things. The focus is on self *and* teacher assessment throughout the study.

Discovering the Concepts

Based on Cohen's Taxonomy for Discovery—experiencing, organizing, sharing, and processing

Laying a Foundation

Students use the songs to learn basic information about living things that will be used throughout the unit. Then they take a school-yard inventory of animals and plants.

Constructing the Learning

Student groups collect data about living things, organize the data, and share their findings with other groups. In a class discussion, they reflect on the experiences and begin to generalize. In this study, students form groups to study a particular living thing of their choosing. Along with their own inquiries, students focus on the living thing's needs and functions, place in the food chain, and adaptations to its environment. Ideas and suggestions are provided for outdoor or indoor activities.

Creating a Context

The play (page 106) creates a context by focusing on living things in a seaside environment. The story invites students to imagine themselves as one-celled animals, plants, and birds. Students review the needs of living things and their functions as they become more aware of the unity of life.

Deepening the Learning

Multiple intelligence activities create real-world and personal connections to the material (page 110). Students write eco-mysteries, design a schoolyard habitat, sing five songs that cover the key ideas, and observe nature in a Solo Spot.

Background

This is a rationale for the hands-on, minds-on, and hearts-on approach to science used in this book. For years teachers have seen the value of hands-on science that gives students opportunities to be active learners rather than just passive onlookers. Out of those experiences came the realization that students need to learn to process those hands-on experiences—thus the term "minds-on science." The history of science makes it clear that good values, including a sense of responsibility, are of paramount importance in science. I call this focus "hearts-on science." Why don't many students experience a true connection to the natural world? How can we help them experience it?

Most children don't have many opportunities to play freely outside, as was common a generation ago. The woods and fields have been covered over with houses and malls. Children are driven to school; their lives are filled with scheduled activities, television, and computer games. Although children are knowledgeable and care deeply about faraway issues, such as deforestation of the tropical rain forests, they have little experience with or knowledge of the natural world in their own neighborhoods.

Cultural norms keep children away from connecting with nature, too. In *Taking the Icks and Yuks out of Science,* science teacher Mildred Ballou (1986) tells of two little girls who were disgusted at the sight of a live mussel inside of a shell. Ballou points out to the girls that "Ick people" can't be good mothers, doctors, nurses, veterinarians, or scientists because all those endeavors involve some "ickiness." "Ah, Oh, and Wow people," however, have a world of opportunity open to them. Girls are particularly susceptible to the ick factor and, as a consequence, are excluded from many science opportunities. Mae Jamison, the first African American woman astronaut, pointed out in a July 1998 interview on National Public Radio that even though women have at least half the brain power in the world, only 10 percent of the people who hold Ph.D.s in natural science and engineering are women.

Some researchers assert that middle childhood may be a crucial time for people to bond with nature, just as six months through six years is a crucial time for children to develop speech. Stephen Kellert (1995) states that human beings' brains are "hard-wired" to relate with natural environments just as the brain is "hard-wired" to relate with other people. Much research has been done on children who fail to bond with other people. What happens to children who never have a chance to bond with nature? And what happens to the Earth we depend on for sustenance when its inhabitants fail to bond with it?

Mildred Ballou (1986) points out that 85 percent of elementary teachers are women. Given some exposure to science studies, students of both sexes show more interest than the vast majority of their teachers. Teachers can do a great service to their students and society by coming to terms with their own "icks and yuks" so that they can turn them into "oohs and ahs" for their male and female students alike. The benefits can be more than academic. When students have a sense of wonder and feel a visceral connection to the living things they are studying, they naturally begin to experience themselves as stewards of Earth rather than mere consumers of it.

This study of living things and the next on monarch butterflies are designed to give students opportunities to develop or enhance their brain's hard wiring through natural experiences. It involves getting beyond negative cultural attitudes that students and teachers may have acquired and into the wonder and beauty to be found in the most ordinary living things around them.

Activities give students opportunities to connect with the natural world in their own schoolyards and neighborhoods. Such opportunities can make for far deeper connections with greater impacts than an occasional field trip to a beautiful natural spot that is divorced from their daily lives. Even in urban settings, a lowly dandelion poking up through the asphalt or a pigeon bobbing its head as it walks around the playground can become rich subjects for understanding and appreciating the natural world.

I have chosen to make this an all-encompassing study—to get to the unity of living things instead of fragmenting the subject into plants, animals, food chains, and so on. Such unity helps students to see the connections. In the discovery section, students engage in concrete experiences and collect data (experiencing). Then they look for patterns and organize the data. Next they share their findings with others, and finally, they reflect on the learning. The study provides opportunities for students to delve deeply into their own inquiries—carefully observing particular plants and animals over time. Observations lead to new questions. The goal is to lead students naturally into developing the skills and motivation to answer the questions. Skills include designing experiments to test their hypotheses, researching in books and on the Internet, and talking with experts, among other things. As understanding increases for students, the desire to preserve and protect the living things around them may also increase.

Domain Matrix

The domain matrix is a tool to help you assess the alignment between stated objectives and activities. You may want to add other objectives to those I have included to suit your own class. You might include, for example, objectives in other subjects or social skills, such as leadership and cooperation. Adapt the activities to help you achieve those objectives. For more information about domain matrices, see page viii.

Activities and Assessments	Outcomes and Objectives								
	Research	Scientific Inquiry	Problem Solving	Teamwork	Needs	Functions	Adaptations	Food Chains	Stewardship
Discovering	X	X	X	X	X	X	X	X	X
Plays and Stories					X	X	X	X	X
MI Activities	X	X	X	X	X	X	X	X	X
Think Trix			X		X	X	X	X	X
Journal	X	X	X	X	X	X	X	X	X
Portfolio	X	X	X	X	X	X	X	X	X
Performance Task	X	X	X		X	X	X	X	X

Objectives

- Students will develop skills in research, scientific inquiry, problem solving, and teamwork
- Students will understand the needs of living things, including the need for food, water, air, and space to live
- Students will understand how living things function, including growth, reproduction, and death
- Students will understand adaptations in living things, including body structures and behaviors
- Students will understand food chains
- Students will see themselves as stewards of the Earth, giving them a sense of responsibility for living things and the environment

Activities and Assessments

- Schoolyard Inventory of plants and animals, including organizing data and comparing findings
- Adopt a Living Thing, in which student groups choose a plant or animal to observe over time
- A story and play to put students' discoveries into a larger context
- Multiple intelligence activities to deepen understanding
- Think Trix questions to encourage students to think about the issues
- Journals to record students' findings and reflections
- Portfolios to collect students' work and reflections throughout the study
- Performance task to see how well students note signs of living things in nature

Getting Ready

- A week or two before beginning, post related words and pictures around the room (see the glossary, page 122). They will pique students' interest and prepare them for new information.
- In their journals, students make Mind Maps of what they know about living things. At the end of the unit, they Mind Map what they have learned, then compare the two maps. Mind Mapping instructions are on page x.

Assessing Understanding

Accurate assessment of student learning is ongoing and derived from multiple sources. The following products add to students' learning as well as measuring it.

Think Trix for the Living Things Study

The following Think Trix questions are examples of the kinds of questions you and your students can use to stimulate different levels of thinking. Formulate and ask these types of questions throughout the unit. Use the icons as reminders to cover each kind of question. See page xiv for more information.

Recall
- What are the basic needs of all living things?

Cause and Effect
- What do you think life on Earth will be like in fifty years? Why do you think that?

Similarity
- How is the life cycle of a plant similar to the life cycle of an animal?

Difference
- What are some basic differences between plants and animals?

Examples to Idea
- Sun, plant, herbivore, and carnivore are examples of what?

Idea to Examples
- Describe three examples of ways living things adapt to their environment.

Evaluation
- In your opinion, is it more important to save endangered plants and animals or allow the local people to improve their economic well-being? Give reasons for your opinion.

Journal

A journal is usually a written collection of reflections. However, journals can also include drawings, songs, and other entries.

  Journaling is one way for students to self-assess, giving them opportunities to integrate, synthesize, evaluate, and reflect on learning. Here are some ideas of what students can do in their journals.

- Mind Map (see Getting Ready, page 96)
- Keep records of their personal inquiries. What questions do they have about what it means to be alive? How can they find answers? What do they observe? What patterns do they find? What experiments do they do? What research sources do they use?
- Record what they learn as in a science log. What do they understand that they didn't before? Which aspects of this subject do they feel they understand? What have they learned about themselves as learners?
- Establish connections between this study and other science studies or other subjects they have studied.
- Note the aspects they don't understand and their next steps for learning about those aspects.

Portfolio Possibilities

A portfolio is a collection of student work that provides evidence of growth of knowledge, skills, and attitudes. Portfolios provide a systematic and organized way for students and teachers to collect and review evidence of student learning over time. A key component of portfolios is a reflection page to go with each entry and with the portfolio as a whole. For more information on portfolios, see page xii. Ask students to include any or all of the following in their portfolios:

- Organization of data from the Hanger activity
- Group and class data from the Schoolyard Inventory
- Notes and organization of data from the Adopt a Living Thing activity
- Schoolyard Habitat plans
- Field Guide plans
- Multiple intelligence activities
- Story of wonder about the natural world
- Eco-mystery notes and story
- A list of living thing adapted to planet
- Photo of poster to protect living things
- Kinds of plants on the lawn
- Comparison of foods animals eat and foods students eat
- Skits for learning vocabulary words
- Data gathered at Solo Spot
- Answers to the Think Trix questions
- Write-up on the performance task—The Living Things Trail

Discovering the Concepts

The activities guide students to discover the concepts. More about this phase and a constructivist approach to learning is on page xiv. This chart shows the steps for the Taxonomy for Discovery. These steps structure the unit for true discovery. A rubric for the taxonomy is on page 148.

Experiencing	**Organizing**	**Sharing**	**Processing**
Investigate. Make observations. Collect data.	Make charts, graphs. Look for patterns.	Compare observations with those of other groups.	What did we learn?

Laying a Foundation

The "Living Things Study" depends on students having some background knowledge about the needs and functions of living things, their adaptations, and the food chain. This activity is designed to give them a beginning understanding of these concepts. The rest of the unit offers students opportunities to expand on these concepts from many perspectives, including first-hand observations of living things.

What's in a Song?

Objectives

- Students will identify some needs and functions of living things.
- Students will understand the concept of plant and animal adaptations.
- Students will understand how a food chain works.

Materials

▶ one copy of each song in this unit for each student (pages 114–118)

▶ other reference materials about living things

▶ CD players

Procedure

Step 1. Divide the class into five groups. Each group listens to a different song.

Step 2. Guide students through the first step of the Taxonomy for Discovery.

Experiencing: Each group listens to and reads the information in the song. They record significant facts from the song and augment their understanding through research with materials in the classroom or in the library.

Organizing: Groups organize their findings into charts and develop creative ways to share the song.

Sharing: Groups share their findings and their creative expressions with the class.

Processing: As a class, students discuss and record the needs and functions of living things. They draw detailed examples of food chains and consider the nature and purpose of adaptations with some examples.

Take a Schoolyard Inventory Activity

Students collect data from the school grounds, a part of the school grounds, or another place near the school. The goal is for student groups to come up with their own ways to take the inventory. This activity leads to a group or individual study of a particular plant or animal over time.

Objectives

- Students develop observation and classification skills.
- Students enhance their teamwork skills.
- Students hone skills in the Taxonomy for Discovery.
- Students do preparatory work for choosing an animal to adopt in the Constructing the Learning phase.

Materials

▶ large sheets of paper

▶ magnifying glasses (optional)

▶ field guides (optional)

Procedure

Step 1. Ask students something like, "Just what have you been walking by every day? You can find out as you take stock of the living things in the area you study."

Step 2. Each group decides on the standards of behavior for its members and a plan for taking stock of what's around them.

Step 3. Guide students through the Taxonomy for Discovery.

Experiencing: Students plan a way to categorize all the kinds of plants and animals that they can find in the designated area. One group could focus on plants, another on animals. Or the whole class could inventory the plants and animals on different days. White sheets or large pieces of chart paper can be helpful in collecting.

Plants

After they have collected samples, you may want to pass out field guides so they can identify their specimens. Students may want to organize samples of each plant on a large piece of paper. They may come up with a different method that is just as effective.

Animals

Students can list the names of larger animals they observe, such as squirrels and different kinds of birds. Finding small animals, such as insects, snails, and worms, may require close observation. Students can look on leaves, especially where there is evidence of feeding. They can look on stems for insects that feed on sap. They can also look on flowers, which are designed to attract insects. They can look on bark and under rocks and logs. They can put a white sheet under a bush or tree, then shake the foliage. They can look along the bottom of windows.

Organizing: The next step is for groups to decide on a way to organize data by deciding on criteria for their categories.

Plants

An important consideration in organizing the data on plants involves distinguishing between examples that are actually different species of plants, and examples that are mere variations of the same plant.

Animals

Students can keep the small critters in bottles or nets long enough to inventory them. Then they should carefully put them back where they found them. This is an important step in showing respect for life.

Sharing: Student groups share their findings, comparing their data and methods for getting and organizing the data with other group's data and methods.

Processing: The whole class decides on a way to compile the data. Students compare and contrast their approaches with the other groups, focusing in particular on the following:

- the methods they designed for doing the inventory
- the data they collected
- their ways of organizing the data

Students reflect on the learning and on themselves as learners. Most people never think about the variety of life around them. Students may well be surprised to find the range of life in the area they are studying. Through this experience, student groups or individuals may find a plant or animal that particularly interests them and that could become a subject of ongoing study in the next phase.

Constructing the Learning

Adopt a Living Thing

Objectives

- Students understand the needs of living things, including the need for food, water, air, and a place to live.
- Students understand how living things function, including growth, reproduction, and death.
- Students understand how animals are physically and behaviorally adapted to their particular environments.
- Students understand the food chain; that is, how living things pass energy from the Sun to plants, which make food, to herbivores (animals that eat only plants) and carnivores (animals that eat other animals).
- Students feel a sense of stewardship: a sense of responsibility for and recognition of the value of living things and the environment.
- Students hone the skills in the Taxonomy for Discovery.

Procedure

Step 1. Review the Taxonomy for Discovery with students. Discuss how students will use it to construct some new understandings about living things.

Step 2. Read the general suggestions about adopting plants and animals (pages 102–105). They include information about some readily available possibilities: dandelions, trees, Fast Plants (plants that grow through an entire life cycle in 35 to 40 days), earthworms, birds, mealworms, and other animals. This section includes two charts with questions geared to study each example. Information on the charts could help students understand what questions to ask when studying other organisms, too.

Experiencing: Groups pick their favorite plant or animal to observe. Along with their own inquiries, the study includes the following:

- What does the living thing need to live? Almost all living things need food, water, oxygen, and a space to live in and reproduce. Green plants also need sunlight to engage in photosynthesis, a process in which they use the Sun's energy, carbon dioxide, and water to make food. While plants release oxygen during photosynthesis, they also use oxygen for their own respiration.

- How does an animal get its food, and who might like to eat the animal? In the food chain, the Sun's energy is passed from plants to several organisms. With each organism, some of the Sun's energy is used up in movement and other functions until it is spent in the last organism at the top of the food chain. When organisms decay, while none of the Sun's energy remains, the nutrients from their bodies may pass on to plants.

- How does the plant or animal grow and reproduce?

- What physical and behavioral adaptations does it have so it can live in its habitat and not somewhere else? Every organism, whether a violet, a vine, a squirrel, or a slug, is adapted to live in its habitat. Just looking at the organism and thinking about it can reveal a lot about how the organism meets its needs. If possible, students will observe organisms in their local environment—on the school grounds, in the immediate neighborhood, or in another nearby place students can visit often.

Organizing: The charts on pages 102–103 list questions you can give students as prompts to help them collect and organize their data. Each chart includes examples that the students might find, with questions about each. If students find other specimens, they can adapt the questions. The chart has a heading for each of the five songs: "Needs," "Adaptations," "Food Chain," and so on. After groups collect information about the living thing they adopt, they agree on a way to organize all their information. Students include how they went about collecting the information and what they found out.

Sharing: Student groups share the information about their living thing with the whole class. They listen to what other groups did and what they found out.

Processing: As a class, they put all the information together on a class chart. Students discuss and reflect in their journals on their findings, including generalizations that are true for all the living things observed. They also discuss ways that human beings can contribute to the well-being of the living things with which they share the planet. Questions such as the following may be helpful:

- What did all the living things your class studied have in common?

- What did you learn about living things' needs, functions, places in the food chain, and adaptations?

Adopt a Plant: Suggestions for Research

	Sample Questions	Dandelions	Trees	Fast Plants
Needs	What does the plant need to live? How does the plant's environment help it meet its needs?	Do more grow close to or far from buildings? Why? On which side of the building do more dandelions grow? Do more grow on sloping or level ground? Why? Do more grow in sun or shade? Why?	What does a tree need to live? How does this tree meet its needs? Has the tree grown away from buildings or other trees? Why?	What helps the Fast Plants grow best? Will students experiment or do research to find out?
Food Chain	How do green plants make food? What kinds of animals get food from the plant? Include this plant in a drawing of a possible food chain.	What kinds of and how many insects visit dandelion plants every day? What animals live in the soil around the dandelion? How do these observations fit with food chains?	What animals visit the tree or live there? Are there signs the leaves have been chewed? Are insects in the bark or on the roots? How do these observations relate to the food chain?	One experiment could be to put the plants on the windowsill. What animals visit? Are they interested in the flowers? How does this relate to the food chain?
Functions— Growth and Reproduction	How does the plant grow and reproduce?	How does each part of the dandelion flower (floret) help make a seed? How many days does each flower take to turn to seed? Add the days and divide by the number of flowers to find the average. How long before the seeds fly away?	What signs of tree growth are there in the spring? Are buds visible? Are flowers visible? Are they green or another color? Do insects or wind spread the pollen? In the fall, the tree's fruit will contain seeds. Does the tree have fruit? How might the seeds spread?	Fast Plants change every day. What signs of growth are visible? What kinds of records can students keep? When do the petals fall off? How long do seedpods take to form? What does the seedpod look like? How many seeds are in each pod? Can they grow?
Adaptations	How is the plant designed to survive in its environment?	How many florets does one dandelion have? If each floret makes a seed, how many seeds would that dandelion make? Count the dandelion flowers in the ground. If each dandelion had the same number of seeds as the one you counted, and all became plants, how many new plants would grow? Why is this an adaptation?	How does each part of the tree help it live in its environment? How does the bark help the tree? How do the roots help the tree? How do the leaves and branches help? Some plants are phototropic; they bend toward the sun. Does the tree bend toward the sun? What other adaptations are there?	Bees and Fast Plants are symbiotic—they are adapted to help each other. Fast plants have pollen that is too sticky and heavy for the wind to carry. How might Fast Plants and bees help each other? How does the flower's bright color help?

Adopt an Animal: Suggestions for Research

	Sample Questions	Birds	Earthworms	Mealworms
Needs	What does the animal need to live? How does the animal's environment help it meet its needs? Is its breathing visible? How does it move?	Do the birds keep coming to the same area? How does this bird find food? How might it find water? Is its home visible?	Find some earthworms (see page 105). Where are most earthworms? How does that place meet their needs better than others?	To find out about the mealworm life cycle and how to buy them, see page 105. What body parts are visible? How does the meal-worm meet its needs?
Food Chain	Is this animal an herbivore, a carnivore, or an omnivore?	Draw a food chain. What does the bird eat? What might eat the bird? Where does the Sun fit in?	Draw a food chain that includes an earthworm. What does it eat? What might eat it?	Mealworms are sold in pet stores for food. What kind of animal might eat a mealworm? Draw a food chain that includes mealworms.
Functions—Growth and Reproduction	How does the animal grow and reproduce?	What kinds of materials does the bird use? Does the male help? Is it possible to observe nests? It is important not to disturb nests or the young may die.	In the spring, in the soil, can you find egg sacs that look like hens' eggs with 8 to 16 eggs inside? Are there tiny, whitish worms in the eggs?	One female can lay 500 eggs. Are there tiny mealworms visible in the meal? Mealworms shed their skin many times in their lives. Are shed skins visible? Why might they shed their skins?
Adaptations	How do the animal's body and behavior help it live in its environ-ment?	What kind of food is this bird's beak designed to eat? What birds with beaks designed to eat a different kind of food do you observe?	How do earthworms improve soil? How do plants help earthworms? The relationship between earthworms and the plants is called *interdependence*.	Examine their legs, mouths, and outer coverings. How do all of these help meal-worms survive? Mealworms can live with very little water. Where are they adapted to live?

- What effective methods for observing and collecting data did you observe other groups using?
- What might you do differently the next time you observe something over time?
- What are some ways that we humans can contribute to the well-being of the living things with whom we share the planet?
- What did you discover about scientific thinking?
- What did you discover about yourself as a learner?

Plants

Dandelions are especially good for study because they are abundant and they change from flower to seed relatively quickly. Each member of the dandelion group could choose a dandelion with several blooming flowers to study over a number of days. By planting mature seeds in pots, students can grow dandelions inside, too, enabling them to keep data on the early growth. The young leaves, very high in vitamin A, make excellent salads.

Trees are interesting to study in and of themselves and also because many other organisms depend on them for food and shelter A group might pick a tree or several trees nearby. Comparing different trees can be instructive. Is the tree a deep-rooted deciduous or shallow-rooted evergreen? Is there a difference in health among trees in the area? Why might that be?

To enrich the outside study, or if going outside is impractical, students can grow plants inside. There are many possibilities, from flower boxes to indoor vegetable gardens. Fast Plants are discussed on the Adopt a Plant chart, page 102.

The "Wisconsin Fast Plant" (or *Brassica rapa)* is related to wild mustard and goes through an entire life cycle very quickly, in 35 to 40 days. Fast plants are hybrids; they are the offspring of a number of different species. Professor Paul Williams at the University of Wisconsin bred Fast Plants originally to help speed up his research on plants. If students or teachers have any problems or questions about Fast Plants, they can visit the Web site www.fastplants.cals.wisc.edu or call a special phone number at the University of Wisconsin, 1-800-462-7417. You can get Fast Plant seeds through the Carolina Biological Supply.

There are many ways to collect data on Fast Plants. Different groups of students could experiment with different ways to care for the plants. Dried bees are available from Carolina Biological Supply for students to pollinate Fast Plants. Students rub the bee's fuzzy body against a flower to pick up pollen. Then students rub a bee's body against the flower on another plant. This may require some students to start over from scratch in raising the seeds. Information on optimal conditions for raising Fast Plants can be obtained at the web site above. In comparing the results, students discover for themselves successful ways to help the plants meet their needs.

Animals

Some students may prefer to study animals. Like plants, animals need certain things to survive. Students can obtain information about the needs of the animals they adopt through direct observation and through research in books, online, and from experts. Students write their questions about their adopted animals in their journals along with plans for finding the answers.

An important skill that students need to learn is how to be still and watch for longer than a minute or two. Students look to see if the animal is breathing. They notice how it moves and whether it is eating or going toward food or water. Perhaps they will be able to see where it lives. Students write their findings in their journals.

Earthworms: If the group wants to study earthworms, they need to decide on where they might find some. One way for students to see if they are right is to make a solution that brings earthworms out of the ground without harming them. Fill a clean, gallon-sized plastic milk container with water. Add two tablespoons of dry mustard and shake vigorously. Don't add any more mustard than that or the solution could hurt the earthworms. Students try several different meter-square areas and carefully sprinkle some of the solution on the ground.

Worms need to be in moist soil because their bodies need to stay moist; earthworms breathe air through their moist skin. Earthworms burrow in the moist soil. Dry soil or waterlogged soil can kill them. As earthworms tunnel underground, they eat soil, digesting decaying bits of organic matter within it. At night, earthworms come to the surface and draw leaves and other plant materials into their burrow for food.

Birds: To study birds, the class might take a walk around the block, listing all the birds they can find. If they don't know the right names, they can just describe them; "small brown bird." Students might check a field guide for the birds' names. Students might choose a bird that lives on or visits the school grounds often.

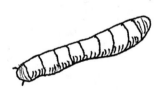

Mealworms: It is easy to find inexpensive mealworms in pet stores. The mealworm container will already have some kind of meal or cereal for the mealworms to live in. Adding a fresh piece of potato every few days will ensure the mealworms have the moisture they need. One way to observe the mealworms closely and regularly is for students to place a few mealworms with a small piece of potato in a petri dish or other small clear container with a top, and place it on their desk. They CD the container to the desk with clear cellophane CD so that they can watch the mealworms and record their activities and any changes.

Over time your students may be surprised to discover that the mealworms are not worms at all, but the larvae of the darkling beetle. The larva will become a pupa. In the pupa stage, the mealworm doesn't eat or move much. Within a month or so, the pupa turns into an adult beetle—white at first, then reddish brown, then finally black. It is also known as a grain or flour beetle because of its food source.

Creating a Context for the Discoveries

BIG PICTURE

Play: Living Things

> *The play gives a big picture overview of the subject matter, including relevant issues and important vocabulary and concepts, without a lecture. Page xx has more information about plays.*

Cast: Narrator; Jennifer, a baby-sitter; Jeremy, a seven-year-old boy; Natalie, Jeremy's five-year-old sister

Narrator: Jennifer, the baby-sitter, is strolling along the beach near the water's edge with seven-year-old Jeremy and five-year-old Natalie.

Natalie: Oooooh, look at the pretty shells! Does the ocean make them?

Jennifer: No, Natalie. Animals made them. The shells were a kind of skeleton, a protection for their soft parts inside! I guess the shell is an adaptation—it helps the animal survive in its environment, the ocean.

Jeremy: Right, the shells are from animals. You've seen Mom and Dad eat clams on the half shell.

Natalie: Yeah, they're all wet and gray and slippery—aghhh.

Jeremy: But what did the clams eat, Jennifer?

Jennifer: Little tiny plants and animals. The clam just sucked them up. Hey, look, kids. That's a food chain. The plant used the Sun's energy to make food. The clam got energy from the plant. Your mom and dad got energy from the clams when they ate them.

Jeremy: I get it! The food chain—the energy goes from the Sun to the plant to the clam to Mom and Dad. Does that make Mom and Dad the predator, and the clams the prey?

Jennifer: I guess so.

Natalie: What happened to the clam that was in this shell? (Solemnly) Did it . . . die?

Jennifer: Well, yes, Natalie. That's what living things do. They are born, grow up, make some new ones like themselves, and . . . die. Dying is a part of life.

Natalie: (Looking up) Do clouds die?

Jennifer: Do they die? What . . . do you think clouds are alive??

Natalie: Of course they're alive. See, they move across the sky!

Jeremy: That's the wind moving them, little Natalie. Besides things don't have to move to be alive. Plants don't move.

Natalie: Well, plants aren't alive.

Jennifer: Let's think about this for a minute. Living things can make new living things like themselves. Can plants do that?

Jeremy: Sure, they make seeds.

Jennifer: Well, lots of them do. Some reproduce other ways.

Natalie: Yes, but plants don't have mouths, so they can't eat!

Jeremy: Plants do too eat! At least they use some of the food they make from the sunlight, the air, and the stuff the roots suck up. They don't need to eat with a mouth.

Jennifer: Some plants even have adaptations that are almost like mouths. Venus's-flytraps and sunbursts are plants that catch insects. The plant pulls the insect inside of a folded leaf and uses it for food.

Jeremy: Wow, I wouldn't want one of those plants to eat me!

Jennifer: Don't worry, you're not their type, Jeremy! Hey, there's another thing living things do—breathe!

Natalie: Watch me hold my breath! I'm gonna get all red!

Jennifer: Don't do that! You need to breathe to live.

Natalie: Okay. I'm breathing again.

Jeremy: Wait a minute . . . Do plants breathe?

Jennifer: Do they breathe? Not only do they breathe, but they make enough oxygen for the rest of us to breathe, too.

Jeremy: Nice of them!

Jennifer: Yes, isn't it? Now, back to Natalie. Living things need water. Do plants need water?

Natalie: Well . . . yeah. I forgot to water my plant . . . and it died.

Jeremy: There, you said it—the plant died, right? So it had to be alive!

Natalie: Okay, okay. But they don't move.

Jennifer: Sometimes they sort of move. See how that pine tree is growing away from the house and toward the Sun? Sometimes plants move by bending toward the sun.

Jeremy: Yeah, but they move r-e-a-l s-l-o-w.

Natalie: Jennifer, what's that black stuff on the sand?

Jeremy: Yeah, its kind of hard and tarry? What is it?

Jennifer: I don't know. Maybe one of those boats out there spilled some oil. Oil spills can hurt the sea life a lot. It gets in the birds' feathers, the fishes' gills, even into the clams and oysters, and kills them.

Jeremy: Yeah, people pollute our earth and make it dirty. Then the plants and animals die.

Jennifer: Pollution hurts people, too.

Natalie: When I grow up, I'm going to clean up the whole world!

Jeremy: Me, too!

Jennifer: Well, you might start with your bedrooms. Let's go home and pick up your toys.

Science for Every Learner, © 2000 Zephyr Press, Tucson, Arizona

Story: Life Mirrors Itself

You may tell stories with rich sensory descriptions and as if the students were actually in the story. Such techniques can help students develop their ability to make internal visual images, which is useful for mathematical thinking and problem solving in general. Stories provide another way to reinforce vocabulary and concepts. For more information about stories, refer to page xx.

The planet Earth is pulsing with the miracle of life. Feel the rhythm of life in yourself with every breath you take. All living things have much in common. Life mirrors itself. Let's see how this is true.

Take in a deep breath and pretend to be an amoeba, a tiny one-celled creature in a drop of water. You are adapted to live, grow, and reproduce in this tiny environment. You are just a blob with no arms or legs or head. You are like Jell-O that hasn't quite jelled. Float about, moving up and down in the water. Take in oxygen through your cell membrane and let out carbon dioxide.

Hey, you sense there's a piece of food ahead of you. Start moving toward the food. Feel part of yourself bulge toward the food; it becomes something like a blobby arm or leg. The rest of you follows and flows into the blobby arm. You get close to the food, and two blobby parts of you trap the food and pull it into you. (Gulping sound)

Another piece of food is ahead of you, but this one is moving faster, so you move faster to catch up to it. Ah, you reach it, enclose it, and gulp it. You are growing bigger. You are taking in water with the food and absorbing water through your skin. You are getting very full. You let out a little bubble of water as waste.

More food is ahead of you. Move toward it, entrap it, and gulp it down. You are growing very big. Will you burst? No. Instead pull yourself into a little ball and become very still. Something deep inside of you is happening. Feel your center getting longer and pulling apart. It divides and moves to opposite ends of you. Feel yourself split in two. Now there are two cells. You have reproduced yourself.

That drop of water you live in is sitting on the leaf of a plant. Now become the plant.

You are a dandelion. Feel your deep, thick taproot reaching into the Earth, taking up water and nutrition from the soil. Earthworms are tunneling under the ground near your roots. The earthworms are keeping the soil loose around you. By the way, that taproot is an adaptation to help you survive. If you get mowed down, that root will let you grow right back.

The Sun is shining light and warmth on your leaves, providing you with energy to make food and oxygen. Hmm, notice that insect chewing a little hole in your leaf? Fortunately, you make enough food to feed yourself and others. Your yellow, many-petaled flower is actually a cluster of flowers or florets held together. Look, the dandelion is changing into a ball of seeds. Each one has a parachute to ride the wind. Here comes the wind now. Whhhhhhhh. Your seeds are spreading, ready to grow in new places. You have reproduced yourself!

Now you are a bird. You are breathing fast, and you are hungry. Swoop down and catch that insect sitting on the dandelion leaf. As you swallow the insect, a little bit of the Sun's energy passes from the plant to the insect to you—a food chain! Your mate is sitting on the eggs in the nest you both built. You are adapted to help her feed the babies when they hatch. Fly back to the nest and see the wide-open mouths of your offspring, begging for food. You have reproduced yourself—and your work has just begun.

Now become yourself. Imagine walking outside, right by the dandelion reaching toward the Sun, right by the tiny one-celled animal trapping food in the drop of water, right by the bird catching the insect that was nibbling on the dandelion leaf. You are feeling a little hungry yourself, aren't you?

Fortunately, you have an apple in your backpack. Is it yellow, green, or red? Take it out and bite into the crisp, juicy fruit. Breathe in as the apple's aroma fills your senses. Feel your mouth water as you slowly chew, tasting that delightful combination of sweet and tart. As you swallow that piece of apple, a little bit of the Sun's energy that was stored in the plant passes on to you.

Living things all around you are breathing, eating, and growing just as you are. They are adapted to meet their needs in their habitat, just as you are. They are producing new beings like themselves. Maybe someday you will marry and have children, too. Living things need clean air, pure water, and some space to live in. So do you. Living things have a lot in common. Life mirrors itself.

As you bring your awareness back into the classroom, look around. What living things do you see?

Deepening the Learning

Multiple Intelligence Activities

Use a multiple intelligence approach to give students opportunities to develop more links in the brain for deeper understanding and greater emotional ties to the new learning. As students develop real-world connections and practice applying the new knowledge in a variety of circumstances, they enhance their ability to transfer their learning to new situations

Verbal-Linguistic

- Students think of a time when they felt a sense of awe and wonder about the natural world. It may have been when they were very young or sometime more recently at camp, at the beach, in the mountains, or somewhere else. They write down their experience, then read or tell it to others in the class. Students look for what the stories have in common.

- Students write an eco-mystery! An eco-mystery is a mystery story based on a real environmental problem. Finding the cause of the problem becomes a mystery to be solved. In looking for the answer, there are always several dead ends, just as there are in regular mystery stories. The climax of the mystery is when the real cause of the problem is discovered. Following are some guidelines that may be helpful to your students:

  1. Read an eco-mystery by Jean Craighead George (see Book Corner, page 122).

  2. Find some environmental problem around your school, home, or another outdoor area nearby.

  3. As you study the area, write down as much information about the area as your senses can take in. This data can add interesting details to your mystery.

  4. When you find an environmental problem, think of how you can best find out what caused the problem. Would observation, perhaps over time, help? Are there experiments that could help? Do you need to do some research—read books, articles, use the Internet, ask an expert?

  5. Develop the characters. Write a beginning, middle, and end. Read your story to others. Listen to their suggestions.

- Students make a field guide! This activity is adapted from some suggestions in *Science and Children* (March 1999). Diane Galleys and her students at Tope Elementary School published their field guide, *Through the Eyes of Children: A Field Guide to Western Colorado and the Colorado Plateau*. One exciting way that students can share their learning about living things is to make a class field guide.

  1. Your class can use the data they collected in the Schoolyard Inventory.

  2. Students decide whether your field guide will have drawings or photographs. They may need to practice the art of drawing or photography.

  3. Get some field guides and/or a specialist, perhaps from the Park Service or a local university or museum, who can bring some references and help students to identify the plants and/or animals. Students write down the

organisms' Latin and common names, any special adaptations to their environments, places in the food chain, uses, or other information they decide to include.

4. Students decide how to organize the field guide. Will it be organized by area or by kind of living thing? Students put the field guide together.

5. Test the field guide. Have another class use the field guide. They can let your class know if some parts are confusing, and your class can improve them.

6. Students share the field guide with other classes, other schools, and the rest of the community. Students may talk on a local radio show about how your class worked together as scientists.

Visual-Spatial

- Students design a planet and draw a picture of a living thing that is adapted to live on this planet. In the drawing, they show how the planet provides for the living thing's needs. Students write about the planet that they drew and describe how the living thing meets its needs in its environment. They describe how the living thing is adapted to live on the planet, and tell about food chains that their creatures might be part of.

- Students design an advertising campaign to help protect plants and animals in their area. They make posters that ask people to protect the wildflowers in their natural settings or to leave rocks and fallen branches where they are to protect animals' habitats.

- Students start or join a bird-watching club. They find out what is needed in their area to protect the birds' habitats.

Logical-Mathematical

- Students take a hanger out to the schoolyard or to a nearby park. They guess how many and what kinds of plants they can find in the lawn. They put the hangers down on a patch of lawn and collect one example of each kind of plant that they find in the space inside the hanger. They count how many of each kind of plant they find and make a graph. The whole class can get together and make a bar graph using all the students' data. Are they surprised at their findings?

- Students calculate their weight in kilograms. Then they weigh an animal to find its weight in kilograms. The animal could be a dog, cat, guinea pig, hamster, or something else. Students weigh the food they eat in one meal, and the food they feed the animal for one meal. They calculate to find which eats the most per body weight. Students compare their meal/body weight to the animal's meal/body weight. If they can't get a kilogram scale, a pound scale will work just as well to answer the questions.

- Students put a piece of green plant in a jar of water and cut the end off under the water. They calibrate a small jar or test tube in milliliters. They scoop the test tube under the end of the plant. Then they put clay gently around the plant's stem over the opening of the test tube so that no water can evaporate. They record how many milliliters of water the plant soaks up in an hour when the plant is in the sun. They compare this to the amount the plant absorbs in an hour in the dark and speculate on results. They should find that more water disappears when the plant is in the sun since the leaves are using water in the process of photosynthesis. The water evaporates through the plant's leaves in transpiration.

Bodily-Kinesthetic

- Students make a schoolyard habitat and become stewards for the environment.

- Schoolyard Habitats is a program developed by the National Wildlife Fund (NWF). It involves combining two powerful ideas: outdoor education and the restoration of habitats for wildlife. Students develop knowledge, skills, and values as they find out firsthand almost immediately that their efforts to help wildlife can make a difference. Students can observe and compare the numbers and variety of wildlife before and after their work in developing a schoolyard habitat. The message is that their learning and efforts actually make a difference in the world.

To Make a Schoolyard Habitat You Need to Have:

Food: Shrubs and plants that provide fruits and seeds for wildlife all year.

Water: A birdbath, pond, or water dish where the water is changed daily. Take care with its maintenance as bacteria buildup in birdbaths can kill birds.

Cover: Shrubs, rocks, logs, and mulch piles provide homes and places for animals to hide.

Places to raise young: Shrubs, trees, and nest boxes are places where animals can raise their young. The National Wildlife Federation Web site provides suggestions for planning, making, and maintaining a schoolyard habitat. NWF also has applications for certification. Join schools all over the country to help. At NWF's Web site (see page 121) students can learn more about the Schoolyard Habitats program and download an application.

- Students role-play a food chain. The group decides on a habitat for the role-play. Some examples of habitats are a temperate forest, a rain forest, an ocean, a pond, and a desert. The role-play will show the energy transfer from the Sun to a plant to an herbivore to a carnivore. They let the carnivore die. As the carnivore's body decays, it sends its nutrients to the plants.

- A group of students becomes an animal, each person acting out the animal's parts. One member of the group describes this animal's adaptations to help it live in its environment. The rest act out the adaptations.

- This activity is from teacher Michael Lausch of Mount Joy, Pennsylvania. In a natural area, groups of three students build an animal shelter. They use only the natural materials in the area. Examples of shelters Michael's students made included a hole in the ground, a nest in a tree, and a pile of brush on the ground. The class travels from shelter to shelter as each group identifies an animal that might have lived in the shelter. Then other students suggest other animals that may have lived there. After the animal identification is complete, each group randomly chooses a card. Each card has a way that people might affect the animals' habitats. Examples are fire, noise pollution, air pollution, and cutting down trees. The groups have five minutes to come up with answers to the following questions:

How might this problem affect your animal in its home?
What can be done to reduce this problem?

Interpersonal

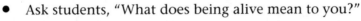

- There are many vocabulary words in this unit. Groups choose words from the glossary at the end of the study. Each group makes up a skit to show the meaning of the words. Other groups guess which vocabulary word is represented. (Note: If the skit shows a misunderstanding of the vocabulary word, then you or other class members can help the group make their skit more accurate.) The class can review vocabulary words by recalling the skits.

Intrapersonal

- Ask students, "What does being alive mean to you?"
- Students designate special spots outside as their Solo Spots. They visit the Solo Spot regularly, perhaps once a week. They collect data about the Solo Spot, including the weather, the plants, and animals, things that were alive at one time, and things that were never alive. They look, listen, and feel for patterns, and they note changes over time. Students write down questions about their spots. They write how they plan to find out the answers—Observation? Experiments? Research? They record their findings.

Naturalist

- Students make their own herbarium. They collect small pieces of plants. They spread out each piece and carefully press it between the pages of a book to dry. Along with each piece, they include a sheet of paper with information about the plant. As the herbarium grows, students start to look for patterns among the plant pieces. Which pieces are similar in some ways? How might that similarity help those plants adapt to their environments? They might include the date, place, habitat, conditions, name, and description of the plant.

Musical-Rhythmic

- Students go outside and listen to the songs of birds. How many different birds can they distinguish? Do they know which birds make which songs?
- Students listen to the following songs on the CD. As they sing along, various parts of the brain help them remember the vocabulary and concepts.

Living Things

What is it that makes something alive? What do living things need? What are some things you can do to help the Earth meet those needs?

From the smallest cell to the tallest tree
Animals and plants are alive like me.
We all need air, some oxygen to breathe,
Water and food and a place to be.

Refrain:
Hey, it's great to be alive!
The world is our home. It's a home to share.
Hey, it's great to be alive!
Let's show the Earth we care.

Every living thing can grow
And reproduce itself, you know.
And death is something living things must face,
So new generations can take their place.

Almost every living thing
Needs water pure and air that's clean.
Soil and sun to make a little food
And space to live with their growing brood.

Refrain

Each of us must have the heart
To care enough to do our part.
And look for ways to save, not waste,
So we all can live in a beautiful place.

There are so many yellows and purples and greens,
We should all be as happy as kings and queens.
Bees and birds and flowers on the ground—
They help us know that love is all around.

Refrain:
Hey, it's great to be alive!
The world is our home. It's a home to share.
Hey, it's great to be alive!
Let's show the Earth we care
For ourselves and each other and the Earth we share.

Words and music by Kathleen Carroll. Singers: The Brain-Friendly Chorus. Solos: Gwen Jenifer, Chialin Chang.

The Story of a Plant

As you listen to the song, follow each stage in the life cycle of a plant. Why do you think it is called a cycle? What are some aspects of nature that help the plant? How does the plant help other forms of life?

From seed to seedling, see the shoots—
Tiny leaves and tiny roots.
With rain and sun the stem grows tall.
The leaves make food which helps us all.

Refrain:
Oh, what a beautiful thing—
The way that plants can grow—and grow!
Oh, what a beautiful thing—
A lovely story to know.

The flower has nectar for the bees.
The bees bring pollen to make seeds.
The petals fall. The flower dies,
So fruit and seeds have space to rise.

Refrain

The seeds will snuggle deep in Earth.
The rain will help new plants give birth.
From seed to seedling, see the shoots—
Tiny leaves and tiny roots.

Refrain

With trees and grass and clover,
The violet and the rose—
Over and over and over
That lovely story goes.

Refrain

From seed to seedling, see the shoots—
Tiny leaves and tiny roots.
See them growing in the rain,
Over and over again.

Refrain

Words by Kathleen Carroll. Music by Joe Brady. Guitar and voice by Joe Brady. Violin: Nick Kendall. Chorus: Gwen Jenifer and Mary Khananayev.

Science for Every Learner, © 2000 Zephyr Press, Tucson, Arizona

The Dandelion Song

People have carried many plants from one continent to another, sometimes on purpose, sometimes by accident. Why would people have carried the lowly dandelion for thousands of miles to their new homes? Is a dandelion flower only one flower? What is special about its leaves and seeds?

Refrain:
Oh, Dandelion! You're more than a weed.
Got the tooth of a lion—and a parachute seed.
Oh, Dandelion! You're more than a weed.
Got the tooth of a lion—and a parachute seed.

When they came by boat to America—not a dandelion was here.
So they brought some seeds to their new land, and this is why, my dear.
The settlers used the leaves for soup, and flowers for some wine.
They made some coffee from the roots. So, thank you, Dandelion!

Refrain

When Frenchmen saw the lion-tooth leaf, they called it *dent de lion.*
The English thought they said *dandelion.* I guess they heard it wrong!
Most people want their lawns bright green. They only want the grass.
But dandelions hold nitrogen. They'll green it up real fast.

Refrain

The plant will grow a yellow bud which opens to the sun.
It looks like just one flower but—there's many in the one!
Each dandelion's a composite scrunch of flowers gently growing.
Its seeds grow in a puffball bunch which wind may soon be blowing.

Refrain

Hold the seed ball to the sun. It's such a pretty sight!
Then make a wish when you are done and—whhh—with all your might!
And watch the little parachutes afloating in the air.
Each one can make a brand new plant—and you helped put them there!

Refrain

Words and music by Kathleen Carroll. Singers: The Brain-Friendly Chorus. Solos: Mary Khananayev, Joe Brady, Ruth Turner, Yan-fang Parsons.

Adaptations

How is a living thing affected by where it lives? Is an adaptation always about how a living thing's body is designed? Can it refer to behavior, too? The adaptations described below help the animals and plants in different ways. What are they? How about adding some stanzas to the song with adaptations of other animals?

Refrain:
Every living thing is adapted to the place where it's meant to be . . .
From the field to the forest to the salty sea
It's adapted to the place it's meant to be.
Adaptations help them live in their environment.
Adaptations help them live in their environment.

The polar bear has long white hair
And a large black nose he covers up with the snow.
He can hide that way when he's stalking his prey.
It's been an adaptation for many bear generations.

There's a father frog who keeps his polliwogs
In his mouth! This family lives down south
In the rain forest—that frog can't get any rest.
But his kids just say their dad's adapted that way.

Refrain

There's a Venus's-flytrap who gets her food with a snap
Of her jaws! This plant makes up her own laws.
In a boggy spot—nutrients it has not.
So she tricks that fly because he's her kind of guy.

There's a butterfly who can get by in the sky
'Cause surprise! Her wings look like two scary eyes
Of an animal who has a very large size.
It's an adaptation that helps her to survive.

Refrain

Now the human race adapts most any place.
Food, water, and air we can bring anywhere.
From the arctic snow down to the jungles we go.
Or to a race in space. We can adapt any place.

Words by Kathleen Carroll. Music by Gwen Jenifer. Singers: The Brain-Friendly Chorus. Solos: Chialin Chang, Joe Brady, Ruth Turner, Michelle Jackson.

Science for Every Learner, © 2000 Zephyr Press, Tucson, Arizona

Food Chain

Listen to this song to find the secret of energy on this planet! How does this energy get used? Follow the food chain along plants and animals in the ocean and in a fast food restaurant. How might this transfer take place in a forest?

Refrain:
'Round and 'round the energy goes; 'round and 'round in the food chain.
The Sun is the source of the energy that goes around in the food chain.

The Sun is the source of the energy in you and me and everything we see.
And green plants store Sun's energy as food so living things can be.
(Spoken) The energy goes—
From the Sun to the plants to the herbivores, who pass the energy to the carnivores.
Then the carnivores die and their bodies decay. They give their energy back to the plants that way.

Refrain

(Spoken) For instance,
The Sun shines its energy to tiny plants called green algae.
Those tiny plants are quite tasty to little fish who need some energy.
The energy goes to a biggish fish 'cause to move and grow is a big fish wish.
So he swallows down that little fish, who makes a very tasty dish.

A giant fish gets energy from the biggish fish swimming in the sea.
Then the giant fish dies and passes energy to the green algae growing in the sea.
The green algae are quite tasty to little fish swimming in the sea.
Every link of the chain, you see, is passing on Sun's energy.

Refrain

(Spoken) Wait a minute!
I don't get energy from the Sun—I eat fast food on the run!
Well—hamburgers that have class come from cows who ate some grass.
The grass stored the energy from Sun to cow to you and me.
The roll, of course, was made from wheat, green plants that store Sun's heat.
The fries from the potato plant store energy from the Sun, you'll grant.

Catsup's from a plant, it's plain. Cokes have lots of sugar cane.
Chocolate's from a plant, the same, and shakes go back to cows again.
The food chain is everywhere, you see, just passing on Sun's energy.
In the woods, in a town, or in the sea, life's passing on Sun's energy.

Refrain

Words by Kathleen Carroll. Music by Gwen Jenifer. Singers: The Brain-Friendly Chorus. Duet: Gwen and Shade Jenifer.

Performance Task for Living Things Study

Performance tasks are products or performances you can use to assess student understanding. Understanding, in this sense, means the ability to apply facts, concepts, or skills to new situations. With performance tasks, the assessment is embedded in the product or performance itself.

The Living Things Trail

Background

You have been learning about living things, their needs, and adaptations. You have also been learning about the food chain, observing and collecting data over time.

Task

Mark a trail on the school grounds or in another place designated by your teacher. Make a map of the area, showing where the trail markers are. Include what the trail markers say.

Purpose

The purpose of the task is to help you understand that living things are meeting their needs all around you. You can find indications of this if you look carefully enough.

Audience

Other students in your class or your school.

Procedure

The trail needs to have signs that show:

- Needs: Indications of an animal home.
- Food Chain: A plant or part of a plant that an animal has been feeding on, with a guess about who has been feeding and where it fits in the food chain.
- Reproduction: A sign of plant or animal reproduction.
- An adaptation of a living thing to its environment. The sign must describe the adaptation.

Draw a map of the area and the trail. Show where your trail markers are and write down what the markers say. To show your understanding, write a paragraph to describe how the trail helps answer the question "What does it mean to be alive?" Include why it is important to take care of the environment.

Format adapted from "A Teacher's Guide to Performance-Based Learning and Assessment" (1996) and teachers of Connecticut's Pomraug School District 15.

Rubric

*A rubric provides criteria and standards for assessing a student's learning. A rubric also serves as a self-assessment tool for the students to use while designing the product or creating the performance. A rubric makes it possible for peers, teachers, and the students themselves to easily calculate a numerical score that represents the quality of the student's performance. **For more information about how to score the rubrics, please refer to number 5 on page xvi.***

Performance Rubric for Living Things Study

Criteria	Blooming Tree	Strong Sapling	Seedling
Needs	Clearly defined sign of animal.	Possible sign.	Not likely.
Food Chain	Clear sign of feeding; logical guess about food chain.	Clear sign of feeding; guess could be more appropriate.	Not likely.
Reproduction	Clear sign, such as flowers, seeds, nest with young.	Possible, connection could be more obvious.	No understanding shown.
Adaptation	Appropriate, clearly described.	Appropriate; could be clearer.	Needs a better grasp of the idea.
Understanding	Clear, complete statement.	One or two parts missing.	Beginning to understand.

Some Places to Buy Materials

▶ For Fast Plants, earthworms, and more:

Carolina Biological Supply Co.
York Road
Burlington, NC 27215
Phone: 919-584-0381

Extensions

Sometimes students' questions take them beyond their ability to observe and experiment directly. The World Wide Web and student trade books offer ideal opportunities for students and teachers to extend their research, often leading to new and better questions, observations, and experiments.

Web Addresses

www.nwf.org

This National Wildlife Federation Web site has information about designing a habitat for wildlife.

www.carolina.com

This is the Web site for Carolina Biological Supply.

www.learningteam.org

This Web site has *Find it! Science: The Books You Need at Lightning Speed,* a CD-ROM with detailed descriptions of hundreds of science trade books.

www.fi.edu

This ask-an-expert service through Franklin Institute Science Museum allows you and your students to receive answers to your science questions from experts in the field.

Book Corner

Books related to the study can do much to spark student inquiry. In addition to science books, include biographies, fiction, poetry, dictionaries, encyclopedias, and other types. Create a center in the classroom with books, pictures, photographs, magazines, and CDs. Here are a few possibilities:

Carroll, Kathleen. 1999. *Sing a Song of Science.* Tucson, Ariz.: Zephyr Press.

This book has stories, raps, songs, activities, and addresses of Web sites about plants and animals, including their interrelationships in the tropical rain forest. Includes a CD of the stories, raps, and songs.

Docekal, Eileen. 1989. *Nature Detective: How to Solve Outdoor Mysteries.* New York: Sterling.

Students learn how to use nature's clues to discover what the mysterious visitors who tromp through the backyard might be. A good source of ideas for eco-mysteries (see page 110).

Doris, Ellen. 1994. *Ornithology.* New York: Thames and Hudson.

Hands-on activities for students to do the work that bird scientists do. Students identify birdcalls, interpret behaviors, discern migration patterns, and more.

Gay, Kathlyn. 1993. *Caretakers of the Earth*. Hillside, N.J.: Enslow.

True stories about students and others who have helped improve the environment. Resources and suggestions for shopping smarter and organizing environmental campaigns.

George, J. C. 1993. *The Fire Bug Connection: An Ecological Mystery*. New York: HarperCollins.

A mystery story that teaches scientific processes and concepts. Can serve as a model for eco-mysteries (see page 110).

Ingram, M. 1993. *Bottle Biology*. Dubuque, Iowa: Kendall-Hunt.

Provides a variety of ways students can learn about living things in a terrarium.

Muller, Gerda. 1994. *Around the Oak*. New York: Penguin.

A fictional story about Nick and his cousins, who visit an old oak in the woods, and the animals and plants that benefit from the tree in each season.

Pascoe, Elaine. 1997. *Earthworms*. Woodbury, Conn.: Blackbirch Press.

Describes how to collect and care for earthworms, how they move and reproduce, experiments, and more.

Glossary

An important part of science literacy is learning the language of science. Classrooms with posted words, stories, and games make learning vocabulary easy and fun.

adaptation: a behavior or physical attribute that helps an organism live in a particular environment

camouflage: the natural coloring of an animal that enables it to blend in with its surroundings

carnivore: an organism that eats flesh

deciduous: a tree that sheds its leaves each year

diversity: a variety of kinds

environment: the physical surroundings in which an organism lives

food chain: a series of organisms, each dependent on the previous as a source of food

habitat: the natural home of an organism

herbivore: an animal that feeds on plants

interdependence: the reliance that organisms in an environment have on one another

organism: a living thing

predator: an animal who hunts other animals for food

prey: an animal who is hunted and killed by other animals for food

seedling: a young plant growing from seed

symbiosis: an interaction of organisms living in close physical contact, usually to the advantage of both

transpiration: the evaporation of water through a plant's leaves

Teacher Reflection

There is no need for teachers to know all the answers. One of the best things you can do for students is to serve as a model of a life-long learner. Use this reflection page to record some of your new understandings as you complete this unit.

What are some of your new understandings in regard to teaching and learning about this subject?

What in this unit worked for your students?

What were some problems that arose?

How could you overcome those problems next time?

What are some other things you would like to remind yourself about this study for next time?

Monarch Study

Ambassadors for Nature

National Science Education Content Standards

As a result of the activities, all students should develop

- abilities necessary to do scientific inquiry   (standard A)
- understanding of the characteristics of organisms   (standard C)
- understanding of reproduction of organisms   (standard C)
- understanding of life cycles of organisms   (standard C)
- understanding of adaptations of organisms   (standard C)
- understanding of organisms and environments   (standard C)
- understanding of the roles of science and technology
  in society   (standard E)
- understanding of the impacts of changes in environments   (standard F)

The Monarch Study at a Glance

Big Questions

The essence of the study, through which all the objectives, activities, and assessments are aligned:

- What makes a monarch butterfly a miracle of nature?
- How does a living thing interact with its environment?

Domain Matrix

A tool to check the alignment of objectives with activities and assessments (page 129).

Time Frame

From a few weeks to a few months in the early fall and into the spring, depending on your schedule and goals

Assessing Understanding

Portfolios and journals are ongoing projects. Think Trix questions assess student understanding and thinking skills along the way. The performance task with rubric culminates the study when students collect scientific data on monarch butterflies. The focus is on self *and* teacher assessment throughout the study.

Discovering the Concepts

Based on Cohen's Taxonomy for Discovery—experiencing, organizing, sharing, and processing

Laying a Foundation

Students use a variety of sources to find out as much as they can about monarch butterflies.

Constructing the Learning

Student groups experience monarchs by collecting data, organizing the data, and sharing their findings with other groups. In a class discussion, they process their experiences by reflecting on them and beginning to make generalizations. Students may study the monarch's life cycle outside or in the classroom. They may keep records of milkweed conditions, tag monarchs, and keep records of monarchs' flight patterns or size and mass as scientists do.

Creating a Context for the Discoveries

The play (page 138) is about some students who watch a monarch's life cycle from egg to larva (caterpillar) to pupa (chrysalis stage) to adult butterfly. The story (page 140) tracks the butterfly's migration across the United States to its wintering site in Mexico, then north again to lay its eggs in the spring.

Deepening the Learning

Multiple intelligence activities create real-world and personal connections to the material (page 142). Students partner with students in Canada, the United States, and Mexico to exchange paper monarchs to simulate the migration. Students pretend to be members of various interest groups near a village in Mexico who are deciding the fate of a monarch roosting site.

Background

The monarch butterfly's migration is a natural wonder of the world. Currently many millions of monarchs fly south from central and eastern Canada and the United States to overwinter in Mexico. (An equivalent feat would be for a six-foot- tall human to travel around the Earth eleven times.) Mysteriously, the following year, those monarchs' great-grand-children, by instinct alone, find their way back to the same roosts in the mountains of Mexico.

Because of the impact humans have on the monarchs' habitats, particularly the milkweed that monarchs live on exclusively in their caterpillar stage, this migration has been called "an endangered phenomenon." Threats to monarch survival may increase because of a genetically engineered corn that kills the corn borer. Poisonous pollen from this corn covers the milkweed that grows near cornfields. This pollen has been found to kill monarchs in laboratory tests. Some scientists believe that unless humans drastically change their impacts on monarch environments, the monarchs' migration may end in the next decade.

Paul Runquist of Monarch Magic has called the monarchs "ambassadors for nature" because these butterflies have inspired a love of nature in so many people. In this study students will learn about this natural wonder and ways people are working to save the beautiful monarch butterflies.

The students' main focus will be to collect data on the life cycles and migrations of monarchs as well as the state of plants on which monarchs depend. Such activities will give students a firsthand experience with ecology, the study of relationships between living organisms and their environments. Students also consider how the actions of humans positively and negatively affect the survival of the living things around them.

In the Monarch Study, students learn scientific concepts and processes by doing research. Engaging in research that has real-world significance motivates students, since they want to feel that they are making a worthwhile contribution. The value of this research increases as it gives students opportunities to develop higher-level thinking skills. Students will design their own ways to organize the data they collect. They will compare their organization methods with those of other students, reflect on their results, and begin to develop theories based on the data.

Good things happen when students think deeply about the data they collect. On the one hand, they develop scientific and mathematical thinking skills. On the other, they provide scientists who are dedicated to helping the monarchs with high-quality data.

Students can easily find monarchs in most areas. Monarchs have been seen in every state in the United States.

The monarch population west of the Rockies is only 10 percent of the size of the eastern monarch population and migrates to the California coast rather than Mexico. The California coast has more than one hundred roosting spots. Recently some west-of-the-Rockies monarchs have been spending the winter on golf courses rather than in their traditional roosts. If owners of the golf courses avoid spraying their plants with pesticides, these butterflies may do well.

Although monarchs are native to North America, their populations have spread, perhaps due to the invention of the steamship in the 1840s. Many scientists believe that monarchs "stowed away" in the holds of steamships that were carrying milkweed for commercial purposes. In 1938, Frank Urquhart was the first researcher to tag monarchs. His work made it possible to find the monarchs' overwintering sites in Mexico in the 1970s. Urquhart notes that monarch butterflies have been found in New Zealand (where the native people, the Maori, call them "Kakua") and Australia, where they have a short migration. Monarchs are also in the Canary Islands, Spain, and on an island off the coast of Africa. There is a white subspecies of a monarch that lives in Hawaii. And monarch butterflies live in

South America all the way down to Argentina.

Milkweed is essential to the monarch butterfly since it is the only food of the larvae. In some ways humans have helped the monarch by increasing the growth of milkweed. Since milkweed grows well in disturbed soil, it has sprung up wherever roads and railroads have been built over the years. In the past, humans' thinning of forests also helped to spread milkweed. However, now milkweed populations are decreasing. The states west of the Rockies are losing 5 percent of their milkweed each year as land that was formerly fields and empty lots is being covered with concrete. However, the primary reason milkweed is declining is that many people consider it a noxious weed and go to great lengths to get rid of it by spraying it with poisons. If this practice were stopped, there would be a net gain in the milkweed population and in the monarch population.

Since finding monarchs in the wild may be impractical in some cases, I have listed several places that provide monarch larvae for educational purposes. A variety of data about monarchs, their migrations, and habitats is available on the Internet, too. The Monarch Study provides students with opportunities to learn important concepts, develop scientific skills, and use those skills to become stewards of the environment. Students also discover how the Internet can provide access to a community of people committed to learning and working together for worthy goals.

milkweed plant

Domain Matrix

The domain matrix is a tool to help you assess the alignment between stated objectives and activities. You may want to add other objectives to those I have included to suit your own class. You might include, for example, objectives in other subjects or social skills, such as leadership and cooperation. Adapt the activities to help you achieve those objectives. For more information about domain matrices, see page viii.

Activities and Assessments	Outcomes and Objectives						
	Research	Scientific Inquiry	Problem Solving	Teamwork	Life Cycle of a Butterfly	Migration Patterns	Interplay with Environment
Discovery	X	X	X	X	X	X	X
Plays and Stories					X	X	X
MI Activities	X	X	X	X	X	X	X
Think Trix	X		X		X	X	X
Journal	X	X	X	X	X	X	X
Portfolio	X	X	X	X	X	X	X
Performance Task	X	X	X	X	X	X	X

Objectives

- Students will develop skills in research, scientific inquiry, problem solving, and teamwork
- Students will understand the life cycle of a butterfly and the monarch migration patterns
- Students will understand the ways in which a living thing interacts with its environment

Activities and Assessments

- Experiences in researching the monarchs' needs, habitats, and migration patterns
- Sharing the data with concerned scientists
- A story and play to put the discoveries students make into a larger context
- Multiple intelligence activities to deepen understanding
- Think Trix questions to encourage students to think about the issues
- Journals to record students' findings and reflections
- Portfolios to collect students' work and reflections throughout the study
- Performance task to allow students to demonstrate understanding by showing they can apply their learning to new situations

---

Materials for Monarch Study
Materials needed will vary depending on the type of studies chosen.

▶ Some useful tools for outside studies might be binoculars, a compass, a watch, a rain gauge, a method for measuring the wind, and a thermometer.

▶ If monarchs are raised in the classroom, many kinds of containers can be used such as mason jars, shoe boxes, or aquariums with netting across the top.

▶ Computers with Internet access, while not necessary to carry on the study, are highly desirable.

Getting Ready

- A week or two before beginning, post related words and pictures around the room (see the glossary, page 150). They will pique students' interest and prepare them for new information.

- In their journals, students Mind Map what they already know about monarch butterflies. At the end of the unit, they Mind Map what they have learned, then compare the two maps. Mind Mapping instructions are on page x.

Assessing Understanding

Accurate assessment of student learning is ongoing and derived from multiple sources. The following products add to students' learning as well as measuring it.

Think Trix for the Monarch Study

The following Think Trix questions are examples of the kinds of questions you and your students can use to stimulate different levels of thinking. Formulate and ask these types of questions throughout the unit. Use the icons as reminders to cover each kind of question. See page xii for more information.

Recall
- What are the stages in the life cycle of a monarch butterfly?

Cause and Effect
- Describe at least three changes that need to take place in the behavior of humans to increase the likelihood that monarch migrations will continue in North America.

Difference

- Read about the viceroy butterfly or another butterfly in your area. Describe some differences between the two. (Viceroys look like monarchs but do not migrate. The caterpillar is different; it is white and brown and actually resembles a bird's dropping. The viceroy has far less of the bitter poison taste than the monarch. Some scientists infer that the viceroy mimics the monarch's color for survival.)

Similarity

- In what ways is the symbolic Monarch Butterfly Migration Program similar to the real monarch migration?

Ideas to Examples

- Describe ways a female monarch might use her senses to find a healthy milkweed plant for her eggs.

Examples to Idea

- The following are causes of what phenomenon?

  ▶ a housing development along the coast in Southern California
  ▶ the destruction of milkweed because it is a "noxious weed" in the United States and Canada
  ▶ spraying pesticides on milkweed and other plants on which caterpillars and butterflies feed
  ▶ the logging of the Oyamel trees in the mountains of central Mexico
  ▶ unexpectedly dry or freezing weather in Mexico from El Niño or other causes
  ▶ a drought that dries out milkweed and monarch chrysalises, reducing the nectar in flowers
  ▶ a spring freeze in the United States that kills young milkweed plants

Evaluation

- Describe some of the possible benefits of collecting reports of monarch sightings from other students on the Internet. What drawbacks might there be in using this source of information?

- Some scientists think it might be harmful to monarch migrations to send monarch eggs and larvae from one part of the country to another part of the country for students to raise in the classroom, then release into the wild. Others think it is safe and helpful. Give several arguments to support each side, then explain your own point of view on the matter.

- Suppose monarchs were unremarkable gray moths. Do you think people would be as interested in saving their migration? Should they be?

Journal

A journal is usually a written collection of reflections. However, journals can also include drawings, songs, and other entries.

   Journaling is one way for students to self-assess, giving them opportunities to integrate, synthesize, evaluate, and reflect on learning. Here are some ideas of what students can do in their journals.

- Mind Map (see Getting Ready, page 130)
- Keep records of their personal inquiries. What questions do they have about butterflies and their migration? How can they find answers to their questions? What do they observe? Discuss? What experiments do they do? What research sources do they use?
- Record what they learn as in a science log. What do they understand that they didn't before? Which aspects of this subject do they feel they understand well? What have they learned about themselves as learners?
- Establish connections between this study and other science studies or other subjects they have studied.
- Note the aspects they need to spend more time on and their next steps for learning about these aspects.
- Draw pictures of the caterpillars and butterflies with the milkweed plants and flowers that they gather nectar from.

Portfolio Possibilities

A portfolio is a collection of student work that provides evidence of growth of knowledge, skills, and attitudes. Portfolios provide a systematic and organized way for students and teachers to collect and review evidence of student learning over time. A key component of portfolios is a reflection page to go with each entry and with the portfolio as a whole. For more information on portfolios, see page xii. Ask students to include any or all of the following in their monarch portfolios:

- authentic assessments of their learning about monarch butterflies in the form of scrapbooks, videos, CDs, or a combination of these media
- a summary of background information about monarchs
- Mind Maps, artwork
- photographs of murals, students at work gathering data, or student presentations
- videos that show students actively engaging in research and sharing findings with others
- videos that document student learning, including the changes observed in the monarch over time; monarchs migrating, collecting nectar, roosting; the conditions of various milkweed plants and the wildlife that depend on them; planting of the butterfly garden
- videos of songs and dances that celebrate the monarch
- research, field notes
- student-made maps of the study area, the garden, and monarch migration routes
- results of any experiments that students perform regarding monarchs, milkweed, or other plants relevant to monarchs
- stories, poems, or songs that students write about monarchs
- CD of song performances

- questions of and answers from the expert at Journey North (page 134) or other places
- symbolic monarch butterfly, with a copy of the note the student sent to the Mexican student, and the note the Mexican student sent back
- reflections on the simulation about the Oyamel Forest
- criteria students developed to check validity of data from the Internet

Discovering the Concepts

The activities guide students to discover the concepts. More about this phase and a constructivist approach to learning is on page xiv. This chart shows the steps for the Taxonomy for Discovery. These steps structure the unit for true discovery. A rubric for the taxonomy is on page 148.

Experiencing	Organizing	Sharing	Processing
Investigate. Make observations. Collect data.	Make charts, graphs. Look for patterns.	Compare observations with those of other groups.	What did we learn?

Laying a Foundation

Researching the Monarchs

Objectives

- Students collect as much information as possible about monarchs.
- Students develop research skills.
- Students acquire background knowledge to prepare them to work with live monarchs.
- Students hone the skills used in the Taxonomy for Discovery.

Materials

- ▶ books, magazines
- ▶ newspaper articles
- ▶ the play, page 138
- ▶ the story, page 140
- ▶ the songs, page 146
- ▶ information from experts

Procedure

Step 1.   In this particular study, you might want to do the play and story first. They will serve as a source for student research.

Step 2.   Students follow the stages of Cohen's Taxonomy for Discovery. For more information on Cohen's Taxonomy refer to page xiv.

Experiencing: Students research in the library, on the Internet, and with scientists, naturalists, and other knowledgeable people for information on monarch butterflies. Research can be about monarch life cycles, habitats, migration patterns, and current threats to the survival of the monarch migrations. Some organizations that should prove very helpful include:

▶ Monarch Watch
Department of Biology, University of Kansas, Halworth Hall
Lawrence, KS 66045
1-888-tagging • www.monarchwatch.org

▶ Journey North
18150 Breezy Point Road
Wayzata, MN 55391
1-612-476-6470 • www.learner.org

▶ listproc@raven.cc.ukans.edu is an online discussion group about monarchs. The discussion group tracks the monarchs' spring and fall migrations, overwintering sites, and recovery of tagged monarchs. It encourages the use of living monarchs for science education and to further student research.

For information about monarchs west of the Rocky Mountains, contact:

▶ Western Monarch Migration Project
c/o Dan Hillburn, Oregon Department of Agriculture
635 Capitol St. N.E.
Salem, OR 97310
1-503-986-4551 • dhilburn@oda.state.or.us

▶ This Web site can also serve as a resource: www.butterflyfarm.com

Depending on where you live and the time of year, students can also look outside for milkweed and for monarchs in various stages of development. They can find monarch eggs and larvae on milkweed growing in parks, fields, vacant lots, school grounds, or their own yards. Monarch butterflies can also be found collecting nectar on a variety of flowering plants in any of these places. Planting milkweed on your school grounds can ensure that you have monarchs to study. If necessary, however, you can also write for monarch larvae to Monarch Watch or Monarch Magic, listed above.

Organizing: In groups, students Mind Map their findings about monarchs, then display the Mind Maps around the classroom.

Sharing: After the class agrees on criteria, each group takes a Gallery Walk to observe each Mind Map for a specified time. Members of the group place "a star/wish/star message" on a self-stick note and leave their message on the Mind Map. "Stars" are appreciative comments about the Mind Map. The "wish," sandwiched between the two stars, is a suggestion for improving the Mind Map. The suggestion is based on some previously agreed-upon criteria. At a signal, groups move on to the next Mind Map and repeat the process. The Gallery Walk is an enjoyable way for students to learn the many facets involved in a study of monarchs.

Processing: In a class discussion, students synthesize their findings, which should result in a basic understanding about the monarch's life cycle, including the necessity of milkweed for its larval stage and the monarchs' migrations to Mexico and the California coast. Include in the synthesis the range of resources students can draw from as they continue their monarch studies.

Constructing the Learning

In the discovery phase, the students become actively engaged in making observations and gathering data about the monarchs' life cycle, habitats, migration patterns, and the effects of particular rearing practices in the classroom. No matter which aspect of monarch research students engage in, the four steps of the Taxonomy for Discovery are relevant.

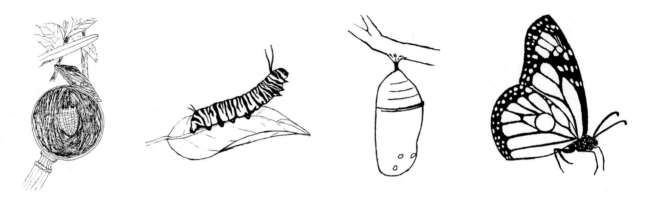

Experiencing: Students begin by observing and collecting information. Following are some examples of observations students could make and record to contribute to monarch research. Students can send the data to the Monarch Lab at the University of Minnesota, Monarch Watch at the University of Kansas, or Journey North in Minnesota.

Outside Examples

- Monarch Lab: Volunteers in the United States and Canada monitor monarch caterpillars, studying their habits in the wild or the condition of milkweed in their area. The area studied can be anything from a backyard or schoolyard garden to a nature preserve, as long as it has an undisturbed area of milkweed. The Web address is **www.mlmp.org/monitoring.html** or contact Karen Oberhauser at **oberh001@tc.umn.edu.**

- Monarch Watch: Tags are provided so the monarchs can be tracked when they migrate. Directions for placing the tags are included. Monarch Watch has several other research projects for students. Detailed information about each project is provided at **www.monarchwatch.org/**. Following are some examples:

  ▶ *Monarch Habits:* In a journal or calendar, students keep records of monarch habits. They record the kinds of flowers the monarchs prefer and don't prefer, and the numbers of mating pairs observed, including the dates and circumstances. Students note the first appearance of migratory monarchs (those with a strong directional flight) and the numbers seen on roosts, perhaps with dates and information about the weather. Some monarch watchers have obtained useful data by counting the number of monarchs that pass a particular site in an hour. Students share this information with the scientists at Monarch Watch.

  ▶ *Flight Directions:* The goal is to give scientists some clues about the answer to the mystery: How do monarchs who have never been to Mexico find their way? Students use compasses to track the directions monarchs take on their migratory flights. While they are outside looking for monarchs, they can look for the following other migrating butterflies as well: Painted Ladies, Buckeyes, Cloudless Sulfur, Orange Sulfur, Red Admiral, Question Mark, Morning Cloak, and Snout Butterfly. You might need to invest in a class butterfly identification book.

▶ *Size and Mass:* Students measure the size and mass of migrating monarchs to find out which monarchs are best equipped to make the journey.

Inside Examples

• Raising Monarchs: Students investigate ways to improve conditions under which monarchs are reared in the classroom. Extensive resources for raising monarchs are available from Monarch Watch for east of the Rocky Mountains.

• First Sightings: Students download data from the Internet on spring and fall monarch migrations that observers have been collecting over the years.

Organizing: The next step in the Taxonomy for Discovery consists of organizing the data. Students look for patterns and group the data they have collected. They present their groupings in charts, graphs, and tables.

Outside Examples

• Monarch Lab: Students might organize their data according to relationships between the condition of a milkweed plant and the survival of monarch larvae.

• Monarch Watch

▶ *Monarch Habits:* Students might look for patterns. For example, they could see a relationship between a date or weather conditions and the number of monarchs they see or the monarchs' behavior.

▶ *Flight Directions:* Students might look for relationships between time of day or season and the numbers and kinds of butterflies they observe.

▶ *Size and Mass:* Students begin to look for relationships between size and mass of butterflies and the size and mass of butterflies north of them.

Inside Examples

• Raising Monarchs: Students might record the number of caterpillars that survive to adulthood under various conditions in the classroom.

• First Sightings: Individual students could search for patterns in monarch migrations in the data they have downloaded from the Internet.

Sharing: Once students have made observations and analyzed the data from those observations, they share their tentative findings with others.

• "Others" may be other students in their class. Students compare their data and analysis of the data with classmates in groups. When students are collecting data on the same phenomena, they can consider together reasons for discrepancies in results.

• When the data are the same, as in the information downloaded from the Internet, students can concentrate on the differences in the analysis of the data.

• Students can communicate with others who share data on monarch butterflies on the Internet. The Internet is a great way for students to share with their own and more distant communities. They can engage in ongoing conversations that compare their data and analysis with those of others on the Internet.

- Students compare the data they have collected locally with those that scientists compile from information sent to them from all over the United States, Canada, and Mexico.

Processing:

- Students reflect on their current skills in observation and organization of data, considering their communication with others.
- Students reflect on whether or not they used the compass or other tools effectively.
- They reflect on their care and accuracy in observing, along with the appropriateness of their individual analysis and organization of the observations.
- Each student involved naturally begins to develop a tentative theory or hypothesis regarding the information as it is collected and organized. If the student discovers in comparing data with others that he or she made mistakes along the way, the student may need to revise the theory.
- Developing a well-thought-out hypothesis is far more satisfying than testing wild guesses. Students may choose to test their hypotheses by using experimental procedures described in Science as Inquiry (page 1).
- Students can judge the adequacy of the data, making sure they send accurate and useful data to the scientists and others who collect them.

Creating a Context for the Discovery

BIG
PICTURE

Play: Metamorphosis

The play gives a big picture overview of the subject matter, including relevant issues and important vocabulary and concepts, without a lecture. Page xx has more information about plays. This play is on the CD. Ask students to consider these questions:

- How can a living thing become something new? What is metamorphosis? What are the changes a monarch goes through on its way from an egg to an adult? Did anyone else in the story have a metamorphosis? What happened there?

Cast: Narrator, Wilbert (a nerdy but wise kid), Heather (a Valley girl type), Ms. Chorion

Narrator: In a field near a school in Maine . . .

Wilbert: Listen, Heather. Listen to the sounds of the insects and birds. There's a little wind blowing through the weeds. The sun feels good. I like getting out of the classroom.

Heather: Well I like to get out of the classroom, too, but not to look at a bunch a bugs. . . . Bor-ring! I'd rather be at . . . the mall—with Josh—than here—with you.

Wilbert: Butterflies aren't bugs; they're insects. Anyway, I think you'll change your mind, Heather. You just need to learn to see. Look. Here's a milkweed plant. Milkweed is the only plant that monarch caterpillars can eat.

Heather: So what? . . . Hey, what's this? A butterfly is hanging under the leaf.

Wilbert: Yes. That's a monarch. Here comes the teacher, Ms. Chorion. Let's show her what we found.

Ms. Chorion: Hi, Wilbert and Heather. Look now. This butterfly is laying an egg and sticking it to the underside of this leaf. In about four days a larva . . .

Heather: A what?

Ms. Chorion: Larva is another name for caterpillar. The larval stage is the growth stage in an insect's metamorphosis—and eating and growing is what larvae do!

Heather: But what is meta . . . meta . . . ?

Wilbert: I know! Metamorphosis. It means change, change of body. Many kinds of insects make a big change during their lives, like the change from a caterpillar, the larva, to butterfly, the adult.

Heather: Yeah, whatever . . . Hey, look. Now the butterfly is flying away!

Wilbert: Yes, and she left this little white egg. It's right there, see? Small as a pinhead.

Ms. Chorion: It seems you two have this situation handled. So I'll go on to the next group. See you later.

Heather: Uh, yeah. See ya later, Ms. Chorion.

Wilbert: Okay, Heather. Now for the monarch log. We need to measure the height and condition of the plant. Hmm, these leaves seem to be in good shape . . . then record the weather . . .

Heather: What do we have to do all that stuff for?

Wilbert: If we send information about the monarchs and their habitats to the scientists at the Monarch Watch Web site, we can help save the monarch migrations. Now we have to remember exactly where this plant is. Maybe we can find the caterpillar when it hatches!

Narrator: A few days later . . .

Wilbert: I'm sure this is the plant. It's exactly forty-three paces from the beginning of the patch.

Heather: Hey, Wilbert, look! Here's the caterpillar crawling along the leaf. The baby is, like, small! It looks kind of grayish-white. You can almost see through it.

Wilbert: It's eating. All they do is eat. In a few days it will grow too big for its skin.

Heather: So then what happens . . . it busts out of its skin?

Wilbert: Right. The monarch caterpillar molts. It sheds its skin. It does it five times.

Heather: Oh . . . Hey Wilbert. Let's give the caterpillar a name . . . Let's call it . . . "Traveler."

Wilbert: Hmmm, Traveler . . . Okay. Sounds like a good name to me. You seem to be getting into this gross, boring bug stuff, Heather. I think you're beginning to get it—there's more to life than shopping at the mall.

Heather: Well, like, hhhh . . . maybe.

Narrator: Two weeks later . . .

Heather: Well, here we are, back to our milkweed plant. Where's Traveler? Look, Wilbert! There's a bird with something in its mouth. Oh my gosh. Did Traveler get eaten? (Frantically) Where is she? Where is she?

Wilbert: Hey. Calm down. Get a hold of yourself, Heather. Here she is, over here in the shade on this piece of hay. See the yellow and black stripes. Look at how big she is!

Heather: Why is she so still? Is she dead? No, wait—she's shivering. Maybe she's cold?

Wilbert: I think she is getting ready to go into a pupa stage. She'll make a chrysalis to change into a butterfly. Maybe we can watch Traveler make the change.

Narrator: A while later . . .

Wilbert: Look! Traveler's skin is splitting!

Heather: Whooa. Her yellow and black stripes are disappearing. Now she's turning green. The chrysalis looks like a green lantern with gold dots around it. This is spooky!

Narrator: Two weeks pass. On the first warm, sunny day after days of rain, Wilbert and Heather return to the chrysalis . . .

Heather: Look, Wilbert! The chrysalis has changed—it isn't green anymore. It looks like a stained-glass window.

Wilbert: Those colors are from Traveler's wings. Now the chrysalis is shaking. The chrysalis is splitting and Traveler is coming out!

Heather: She's all crumpled up. Do you think she's okay? Wait! She's pumping fluid into her wings. The wings are filling out!

Wilbert: Yeah, they'll be dried off soon. Oh, hi, Ms. Chorion.

Ms. Chorion: Good timing, Wilbert and Heather. Now that she's dry, you can tag her.

Wilbert: Oh, yes. That's the tag we got from the scientists. The tag can help researchers find out a lot about how different monarchs migrate to Mexico.

Heather: Won't that hurt her?

Ms. Chorion: Not if you are very careful. You can catch her in the butterfly net, then gently hold her wings together and put the dot on the lower wing.

Wilbert: Okay, there, she's tagged.

Heather: Look at her go. She's flying away!

Wilbert: Whoooeeee! I hope she makes it to Mexico.

Heather: I can't believe it. I still like malls, but . . . thanks to you, Wilbert, I really got into this butterfly. She's just an insect, but . . .

Heather and Wilbert: Traveler rules!!!!

Story: Monarch to Mexico: Traveler's Adventures

You may tell stories with rich sensory descriptions and as if the students were actually in the story. Such techniques can help students develop their ability to make internal visual images, which is useful for mathematical thinking and problem solving in general. Stories provide another way to reinforce vocabulary and concepts. Page xx has more information about stories. This story is on the CD.

This is a sequel to the metamorphosis play. It's about Traveler, the butterfly, crossing a huge continent. Follow her journey on a map. Which states in the United States and Mexico does she travel through? What are some of the dangers a monarch may face in her travels?

Sit back, relax, and allow your imagination to take over. Pretend you are Traveler, the monarch butterfly. You are about to begin a great journey, traveling farther than any other insects in the world. You will spend two and a half months flying from Maine to Mexico.

Notice your new body that will take you on this journey. Like all insects you have a head, thorax, abdomen, and six legs. Stretch out your four black, orange, and white wings attached to your thorax. Feel their power yet delicacy! Use your muscles to move them. You weigh less than a gram, yet these wings and muscles are adapted to carry you thousands of miles.

At this moment, as you fly away from the field that has been the only world you have ever known, all you are aware of is that you are hungry. You must store energy to survive the long journey ahead of you. Using your two marvelous six-sided insect eyes, imagine seeing 72,000 images all at once. As you see bright colors, your antennae smell the fragrance of some late-blooming flowers. Unroll your proboscis, your drinking tube, to sip some nectar from asters and goldenrod by the side of the road. Use your feet to taste the plant's sweet liquids.

You rise again, now over the forests of Maine and New Hampshire, as air currents help you along. As the afternoon grows cooler, come down to a backyard garden of marigolds and zinnias. Now, move from blossom to blossom, and sip your fill, nectaring in the sun to keep your body warm.

It is getting dark. Feel yourself hanging upside down on a branch of a maple tree for the night. Close your wings above your back so only the yellow underwing can be seen. Now, it is the next morning. Warm your muscles in the sun, sip some nectar in the garden, then begin heading south again.

Weeks pass by as you continue your journey down the eastern seaboard. Feel yourself ride the wind! It can help you travel as much as 80 miles before nightfall. Some days you make very little progress, but you fatten up on the nectar from the fall flowers along your path. Despite all your exercise, you will actually gain weight during your trip!

After crossing through Connecticut, you go further inland, avoiding the concrete cities. Finally you reach the southern tip of New Jersey, Cape May. Cape May has a wildlife sanctuary on the edge of the peninsula, a beautiful haven for you and thousands of migrating birds and butterflies that stop here for food and rest.

Just as you are about to plunge across the Delaware Bay, the clouds cover the sun. Crossing large bodies of water can mean life or death. You feel the coolness in the air. If your body temperature gets too low with no safe place to rest, you could easily drown. Will you make it across the bay or will your life end in the cold gray waves? *(Put your player on pause for a minute and discuss how a butterfly might survive this challenge.)*

Your instinct tells you that this is no time for a water crossing. You spend the night safely covered in a bayberry bush near the shore. The next day a warm breeze hitting cooler air creates a thermal, a column of air, which gently lifts you and hundreds of other monarchs for a free ride across the 15 miles of the Delaware Bay to the Delaware shore.

Keep heading west across the fields of eastern Maryland and over the Chesapeake Bay. A seagull flies near you. You don't become part of its food chain, though. Maybe it remembers that monarchs taste terrible, thanks to the milkweed you ate as a caterpillar.

Soon you find yourself above zooming cars, which create false winds. You fly about frantically and manage to pull yourself out of this terrifying whirlwind without hurting your wings. Others, however, are less fortunate.

Down in Virginia, you join thousands of monarchs. Notice yourself swarming with them over the mountains to the hilly forests of Tennessee. Look down as you fly across the wide Mississippi River. It's getting warmer. One day in Arkansas, you are nectaring on a delightful butterfly bush in someone's backyard. People all over the United States and Canada are planting gardens like this one to help butterflies and other wildlife.

You and many other monarchs cross over into Texas and travel down the Gulf Coast. In south Texas, the heat is intense, too intense. Stop now in a shady canyon north of the Rio Grande, and sip on some frostweed nectar. The weather cools a bit, so you begin flying again and soon cross the border into Mexico.

It is getting warmer as you go. A massive cloud of butterflies sweeps into the mountain ranges of central Mexico, wings flapping above, behind, and on either side of you. You have joined thousands of monarchs coming down the central flyway through the middle of the continent heading to a few small roosts in the mountain forests near Mexico City.

You arrive in a roost near El Rosario in a forest of Oyamel fir trees. Rest! You must be warm enough not to freeze, yet cold enough so your metabolism slows down and you can conserve energy. The spot must have water and nectar along with protection from the weather. These perfect microenvironments are called Magic Circles.

Now it is late November. You, along with hundreds of other monarchs, hang motionless with your wings folded back like clusters of yellow leaves on the Oyamel trees. Occasionally your muscles warm up enough for you to fly to a nearby stream for a drink of water.

One December afternoon on your way back from sipping the nectar of some wild sunflowers, a cloud passes over before you get to your roosting site. Feel your body cool; it is getting harder and harder to move your wings. Try as you might, you can't move. You land on the forest floor. You are in danger! *(Pause the player for a few minutes and discuss what the threats might be.)*

First there is the threat of cold. Remember that you, like all cold-blooded animals, can freeze if you are not protected from low temperatures. Also, birds and small animals are waiting in the shadows to eat you.

A stroke of luck! A young girl (one of the ecotourists) happens by and notices that you are still living. Feel her gently pick you up. She excitedly writes down your tag number so she can send your number and location to the scientists with Monarch Watch. Now she breathes warmth on to you. Feel yourself move again! Ahhh. Now spread your wings and fly to your roost. Safe!

It is February. You and the other butterflies open your wings to bask in the warm sun for a while; the Oyamel tree turns bright orange. Now, fly free from your winter roost. You have used up your fat reserves; you are thirsty and hungry. Flow down the mountain with the others. It looks like a river of monarchs. Hundreds of you sip gratefully on the flowers down the side of the mountain. Now it is time for the monarchs to complete their destiny. Whirling and twirling through the air, they begin mating.

By late March your instincts are urging you to fly northeast, hundreds of miles to Texas. Your wings are faded and tattered. You're losing weight; it takes great effort to keep going. But your main mission, to find milkweed, the only plants your young are adapted to eat, urges you on to fields from Houston to Arkansas. Notice the newly sprouted milkweed plants, perfect for your 700 eggs. While it is the end of an extraordinary life for you, you have succeeded in creating a new generation of monarch butterflies.

Spring and summer monarchs only live a few weeks. Some of your young become mature butterflies and continue the northeast journey you began. Their offspring first see light in Virginia, Maryland, and Delaware. Some of them make it back to Maine and the very field where you were born.

One summer day Wilbert and Heather are looking over that field and see a beautiful orange and black butterfly on a flower. "Hey!" they exclaim. "Could that be the grandchild of Traveler?" And it is.

Science for Every Learner, © 2000 Zephyr Press, Tucson, Arizona

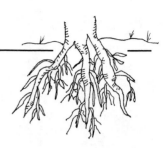

Deepening the Learning

Multiple Intelligence Activities

Use a multiple intelligence approach to give students opportunities to develop more links in the brain for deeper understanding and greater emotional ties to the new learning. As students develop real-world connections and practice applying the new knowledge in a variety of circumstances, they enhance their ability to transfer their learning to new situations.

Logical-Mathematical

- The Biological Clock comes from an activity suggested by Journey North. Migrating animals need to have a sense of time to survive. Cover the clock in the classroom. Ask students to remove their watches. At times, ask students to write down what time they think it is. Students discuss the internal cues (hunger, fatigue) and external cues (school bells, sunlight patterns in classroom, passing buses) they used to make their guesses. Graphing students' estimates could be interesting. Students list ways monarchs might be able to determine time in the course of a day. Students also list reasons it is important for monarchs to be able to know at what time of the day to do certain things.

- Monarch Watch (www.monarchwatch.org) has a realistic story about a monarch butterfly by Marilyn Rugles and Orley Taylor—"Gulliver's Story: An Exercise in Active Learning." In the "active learning" exercise that accompanies the story, students form a think tank to answer questions. The answers are not given directly in the story. Answering the questions requires students to make some inferences based on the information. The goals are to encourage students to develop habits of inquiry and to practice using their knowledge to solve problems.

Verbal-Linguistic

- Students write and illustrate books about monarch butterflies for younger children. Students use this book and other resources to teach younger children about these amazing insects.

- The class compiles questions to write to "Ask an Expert" at Journey North (address on page 134).

- Students write to their representatives and ask for help in raising the commitment for creating and preserving habitats for monarchs in their state or province.

- Students ask their local Chamber of Commerce to use their influence to reduce the spraying of weed killer on roadside milkweed.

- The class subscribes to the online newsletter *Habitats* for backyard wildlife enthusiasts from the National Wildlife Foundation. The Web site is www.igc.org/nwf/habitats/newsletter/v1n3/sy2.html. Some classroom discussions center on topics in the newsletter.

- Students make their own Web site, describing their studies of monarchs for others.

Visual-Spatial

- Students create a mural that shows the life cycle of a monarch and milkweed plants.

- Students make a video that documents their studies of monarchs reared in the classroom or found in the wild.

- Students make a map of North America. They track the monarchs' migration in spring or fall. They might make an overhead transparency from an atlas, then trace the map onto butcher paper with fine-point, felt -tip markers. You can buy commercial maps for the purpose from Rand McNally. Information is provided on page 149 in the Places to Buy Materials section.

- Using the same map, students trace Traveler's route from Maine to Mexico as the story is read. They use a different color from the one they used in the previous activity.

- Students make a map that shows where milkweed grows in their area.

- Students become a part of the Symbolic Monarch Butterfly Migration program, an international partnership between Canada, the United States, and Mexico. Each year more than 40,000 US and Canadian students make paper monarch butterflies to send to Mexico City's Children's Museum in early November, just as the real butterflies arrive in Mexico for the winter. Forty thousand Mexican children watch over the paper butterflies for the winter. In the spring, when the real butterflies begin to fly north, the Mexican children send the paper butterflies with a special message to the students in Canada and the United States who made them. Paper monarchs must be mailed to Journey North, 125 North 1st St., Minneapolis, MN 55401 USA by early October to be part of the symbolic migration. Butterfly patterns, as well as other information, are available at Journey North's Web site: http://www.learner.org/jnorth.html.

Bodily-Kinesthetic

- Students take part in a simulation to make a decision about a forest of Oyamels on a mountain in central Mexico. Individuals or groups of students take on the point of view of different interest groups:

  - Poor villagers who need to cut down the Oyamel trees, even in protected areas, for fuel

  - *Ejidos,* groups of peasant farmers, who own the land as a group and have been required by the government to reduce or eliminate logging but have not been paid for doing so

  - Mexican government officials who are trying to uphold Mexico's presidential decree to protect five of the butterfly overwintering sites. The decree allows for two zones of protection: the nuclear zone allows no cutting, and the buffer zone allows limited cutting.

  - Mexican loggers who consider the wood of the Oyamel trees very valuable

  - Scientists who wish to help keep the monarchs alive

  - Tourists who come to central Mexico to see the monarchs roosting for the winter

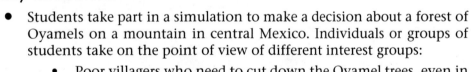

- Students research the points of view of the groups they represent. During the simulation, they speak for their interest group at a meeting set up to decide the fate of the Oyamel forest. Students may decide to dress the part of the groups they represent. After hearing each point of view, students brainstorm ways to meet everyone's needs. Students can share their solutions with Monarch Watch or Journey North.

Interpersonal

- Journey North (www.learner.org) invites young people and adults all over North America to report first sightings of monarch butterflies traveling north each spring. Journey North suggests that classes engage in a conversation that is very relevant to anyone who uses information from the Internet. The topic of the conversation is "Can you trust your source?" Students discuss the probable reliability of Internet sources.

  An obvious example of a questionable source is a message from a kindergartner who claims to have sighted 500 monarchs in Minnesota in February. The kindergartner's teacher said that her students were just beginning to identify monarchs.

  Second-grade students in Jim Hateli's class were confused about a monarch sighting in early April in New Jersey. Other sightings had been in Georgia, Alabama, Kansas, and Missouri. The students decided that the New Jersey report had to be a mistake—until they found out that a naturalist who tags hundreds of monarchs each fall made the sighting.

  Students decide on a set of criteria to determine the trustworthiness of reports. Journey North suggests such criteria as:

  - the observer's level of experience. Does the observer know what a monarch looks like?
  - the amount of time spent watching for monarchs before the observer reported the first monarchs in the region
  - the likelihood that a monarch would be seen at that time in a particular region, given the average temperature and climate

  Students will understand that scientific inquiry includes a review process. In a spirit of collaboration in the scientific community, students can e-mail those who report unexpected findings and respectfully question the observers further.

- Participate in the Adopt-a-Classroom program. The communities around the monarchs' roosting sites are very poor. The schools are cinder-block buildings with few teaching materials. Monarch Watch is committed to helping the communities by helping the schools. For $100, your class can contribute a basic math and science kit for a classroom. If you don't have money, other resources, such as paper, crayons, paper clips, overhead projectors, and musical instruments, are also welcome. When Monarch Watch gets a vanload of supplies, the director of Monarch Watch will see that they are delivered to the schools in Michoacán.

Intrapersonal

- Students pretend to be monarchs. They describe the experience of being an egg; of living as a growing, eating, and molting caterpillar; of changing inside a chrysalis; and of emerging as a new butterfly.

- In their journals, students also explore the feelings, thoughts, and musings that arise.

Naturalist

- Students plant butterfly gardens at school or at home. They ask everyone to notice which kinds of plants in their neighborhood attract the most butterflies. Monarchs and other butterflies love the nectar of asters, goldenrods, marigolds, zinnias, coreopsis, coneflower, butterfly weed, butterfly bush, and sunflowers. Wildflowers native to your area are especially easy to care for since they are adapted to your climate. Check this Web site for more flower options: www.kidsgardening.com.

  Monarch Watch sells a Students' Butterfly Garden Kit. Proceeds benefit the Monarch Butterfly Sanctuary Foundation that helps protect monarch habitats in Mexico.

- Students plant milkweed. Monarch caterpillars eat only milkweed. In some areas, milkweed is available at garden centers. Contact www.monarchwatch.org for milkweed seeds and excellent information about monarchs and how students can help scientists gather new information about monarchs.

- Students follow the progress of monarchs and other migrating animals in North America. They contact Journey North at www.learner.org for information.

Musical-Rhythmic

- *Mariposa* is the Spanish word for "butterfly." Students write a poem or song about the mariposa.

- Students pick appropriate music and create a monarch dance. The dance could mimic the monarch passing through its various life-cycle stages, migrating, nectaring, roosting, and so on.

- Students write a monarch song to a Mexican or Country and Western tune.

- Students listen to "The Monarch Song" (page 146) to reinforce their knowledge of the vocabulary and the sequence of the monarch's life cycle and migration.

The Monarch Song

As you listen to this song, follow the life cycle of this amazing insect. What are its stages in becoming a butterfly? How does the monarch butterfly connect the North American continent?

Refrain:
Butterfly, fly down to old Mexico.
Butterfly, fly down to old Mexico.
Winter ends and then—you will fly north again.
Home to milkweed you'll go.
Winter ends and then—you will fly north again.
Home to milkweed you'll go.

She lays an egg on the under leaf. After four or five days
A tiny larva will hatch. You'll see—on the leaf it will graze.
Caterpillar will grow and grow eating leaves every day.
Then upside down it will hang below in a beautiful "J."

Refrain

A bright green pupa with golden dots where our friend used to be
Turns orange and black dressed with small white spots—a butterfly soon we'll see.
A monarch hatches and dries her wings. Tiny migrant she'll be—
With waves of thousands she'll ride the wind. Marvelous mystery!

Refrain

Monarch millions to Oyamel trees. In magic circles they'll grow
Holding tight now against the breeze, in El Rosario.
When spring arrives, butterflies will mate, flying north for their young.
Three generations—some find their fate in Canadian sun.

Refrain

Words and music by Kathleen Carroll. Singers: Betty Simkin, Ben Carroll, Gwen Jenifer. Percussion: Gil Glass and Nick Kendall. (Nick is keeping the beat with a pair of kitchen scissors and a dinner knife!)

Performance Task
for the Monarch Study

Performance tasks are products or performances you can use to assess student understanding. Understanding, in this sense, means the ability to apply facts, concepts, or skills to new situations. With performance tasks, the assessment is embedded in the product or performance itself.

Background

You have been studying the monarch butterfly with your class and have taken part in a number of activities to learn about the monarch's life cycle, habitat, migration, and the issues that threaten its continued existence. You have collected and analyzed data, and shared your findings. Now you will demonstrate your own understanding of the concepts and scientific processes through independent research.

Task

Do independent research on the monarch that may become part of the data that scientists are collecting. The research you choose will depend on the time of year, the area you live in, and your own interests.

- If it is spring or early fall, you might study monarch life cycles in your classroom or outside. You might study the monarch's habitat, or collect data on the larvae's sense of touch or the percentage of sugar concentrate monarch butterflies prefer. Paul Runquist of Monarch Magic suggests keeping butterflies in the classroom for a few days after they have emerged so you can observe them before setting them free. He recommends hand feeding the butterflies by gently unrolling the proboscis with a cotton swab soaked in a sugar solution.

- Depending on where you live, the fall may also offer opportunities to tag the butterflies or to track the migrations.

- If the area in which you live is an inappropriate place to work directly with monarchs or milkweed, you may choose to analyze the data on the Internet. Perhaps you will notice some important new patterns! There are many ways to contribute.

Procedure

Step 1. Record information and reflections in a journal for this performance task.

Step 2. Work through the stages in the Taxonomy for Discovery.

Experiencing: Make observations and collect information. Write down the information you collect in your journal, being sure to record the date and time you begin and stop collecting data.

Organizing: Show a variety of ways the data can be organized. Organizing the data could reveal a story. Will the data tell the story most effectively in a chart or table? Or does a graph or diagram tell the story more clearly? Record in your journal the methods of organization you try. Put an asterisk next to the organization method you think tells the story best.

Format adapted from "A Teacher's Guide to Performance-Based Learning and Assessment" (1996) and teachers of Connecticut's Pomraug School District 15.

Sharing: Share the information you gathered with two to four other students. Listen to one another's information and write several comments and a suggestion or two for the other students in their journals, signing your name next to your comments.

Processing: Use your journal to reflect on the effectiveness of your collection and organization methods. Discuss your findings with others. As a result of the discussion, reflect on whether you learned about a more effective way to collect data or organize it. Are you satisfied with your work so far? On what do you base your assessment?

Possible criteria that indicate a need to collect and reorganize the data include the following:

- Others collecting data on the same phenomena got very different results.
- Someone points out an error in thinking or in the organization of the data.
- Someone points out a simpler and more elegant way to organize the data.

Rubric

A rubric provides criteria and standards for assessing a student's learning. A rubric also serves as a self-assessment tool for the students to use while designing the product or creating the performance. A rubric makes it possible for peers, teachers, and the students themselves to easily calculate a numerical score that represents the quality of the student's performance. **For more information about how to score the rubrics, please refer to number 5 on page xvi.**

Performance Rubric for Monarch Research

Criteria	Advanced	Intermediate	Beginner
Experiencing	Is fully immersed in the experience. Makes and records many observations.	Adequate involvement. Makes and records observations.	Slow to participate. Makes and records few observations.
Organizing	Records several possible ways of organizing information. Strong rationale for preferred mode. Describes appropriate patterns.	Has at least one option for organizing information.	Beginning to organize information; rationale missing or needs work.
Sharing	Can communicate own findings. Can repeat back others' findings. Perceptive written comments/suggestions.	Can repeat back main idea; some findings missing. Acceptable written comments/suggestions.	Can repeat back a few of peers' findings; comments not written or not relevant to the findings.
Processing	Excellent use of feedback to improve own findings; begins to articulate a hypothesis.	Some use of feedback; may need to overcome tendency to hold on too much to own ideas or give them up too easily.	Beginning to develop ability to think about one's own thinking and to reflect on process.

Places to Buy Materials and Connect with Scientists

▶ There are a number of opportunities for students to partner with scientists in monarch research. Students can increase the likelihood that the monarch migration will continue as they learn important scientific concepts and principles. Following are some resources that make this partnership possible:

Monarch Watch (www.monarchwatch.org)

Out of the University of Minnesota and the University of Kansas, Monarch Watch organizes volunteers across the United States and Canada to contribute data from their regions to monitor monarchs and their migrations. Initiated in 1991, Monarch Watch offers a variety of ways that students can collect research data on monarch butterflies. Currently more than 40,000 students in the United States and Canada are tagging monarch butterflies through Monarch Watch. You can also buy a Monarch Rearing Kit, teaching materials, and four kinds of milkweed seeds through Monarch Watch, c/o O. R. Taylor, Department of Entomology, Haworth Hall, University of Kansas, Lawrence, KS 66045. Their e-mail address is Monarch@ukans.edu. If you live east of the Rocky Mountains, it may be possible to buy eggs and larvae from this address. For Monarch Watch information on tagging butterflies, call 1-888-TAGGING or 1-785-864-4441.

Journey North (www.learner.org)

This site provides an opportunity for people all over North America to use and contribute to a database about Monarch migrations.

Monarch Magic

Monarch Magic provides books, larvae, and eggs to states west of the Rocky Mountains. It also has activity guides, a butterfly abode, posters, books, puppets, stamps, and other materials. Write c/o Paul Runquist, PO Box 7119752, Ashland, OR (541-482-3429).

David Marriott

Marriott has a monarch program and an exhibit, and sells a variety of milkweed seeds and plants and larvae. Look for David Marriott's Web site: www.butterflyfarm.com. The Web site has pictures of different kinds of milkweed and maps of the United States showing the range of each type of milkweed in the wild. Write to David Marriott, PO Box 17871, San Diego, CA 92177 (619-274-6817).

Karen Oberhauser

Oberhauser has excellent curriculum guides about monarch butterflies. Write to Karen Oberhauser, Department of Ecology, 1987 Upper Buford Circle, St. Paul, MN 55108; fax, 612-624-6777; phone, 612 624-8706; e-mail, oberh001@tc.umn.edu.

Volunteers in the United States and Canada monitor monarch caterpillars and milkweed in their area. Anywhere from a backyard garden to a nature preserve is acceptable as long as it has an undisturbed area of milkweed. To register for the program, e-mail a message to: oberh001@tc.umn.edu or write to Karen Oberhauser, Department of Ecology, Evolution, and Behavior, University of Minnesota, Ecology Building, St. Paul, MN 55108.

Rand McNally

For maps to track monarch migrations, contact the Latitudes Map Store. Phone, 612-927-9061; fax, 612-927-9163; or e-mail, Arrowmap@aol.com. If you explain your purpose, they can help you order the best map.

www.learningteam.org has *Find it! Science: The Books You Need at Lightning Speed,* a CD-ROM with detailed descriptions of hundreds of science trade books.

Extensions

Sometimes students' questions take them beyond their ability to observe and experiment directly. The World Wide Web and student trade books offer ideal opportunities for students and teachers to extend their research, often leading to new and better questions, observations, and experiments.

Web Addresses

See specific activities for Web addresses that pertain to them.

Book Corner

Books related to the study can do much to spark student inquiry. In addition to science books, include biographies, fiction, poetry, dictionaries, encyclopedias, and other types. Create a center in the classroom with books, pictures, photographs, magazines, and CDs. Here are a few possibilities:

Brewer, Jo. 1967. *Wings in the Meadow*. London, UK.: J. M. Dent.

> This is a beautifully written story of a monarch butterfly. Although this book was written before the monarch overwintering sites in Mexico were discovered, the author gives a detailed and fascinating description of life in a meadow.

Lasky, Kathryn. 1993. *Monarchs*. San Diego, Calif.: Harcourt Brace, Gulliver Green.

> This book describes the life cycles and winter migrations of eastern and western monarch butterflies. The book also describes the efforts of people in two towns, El Rosario in Mexico and Pacific Grove in California, to save the monarchs' overwintering sites.

Pringle, Lawrence. 1997. *An Extraordinary Life: The Story of a Monarch Butterfly*. New York: Orchard.

> The author gives a firsthand view of and some up-to-date information about a monarch's life cycle, feeding habits, migration, potential predators, and mating. He conveys the information through the life story of a single monarch butterfly.

Glossary

An important part of science literacy is learning the language of science. Classrooms with posted words, stories, and games make learning vocabulary easy and fun.

abdomen: the posterior section of the body of an insect; attached to the thorax

adaptation: body part or behavior that helps an organism survive in its environment

antennae: a pair of moveable feelers on the head of an insect that are sensitive to touch and taste

chorion: the outer covering or shell of an insect's egg

chrysalis: the hard outer case that encloses the pupa of a butterfly or moth as it changes from caterpillar to adult

cold-blooded: having a body temperature that varies with the environment

El Rosario: a village near one of the most famous Mexican roosting sites for monarchs

food chain: a series of organisms, each dependent on the next as a source of food

larva: the caterpillar stage in an insect's life cycle

Magic Circles: clusters of Oyamel trees in central Mexico with just the right conditions for monarchs to roost in the winter

metamorphosis: a change of form, for example, the transformation of a butterfly from pupa to adult, or of a tadpole to a frog

migration: a seasonal movement of an animal from one environment to another

milkweed: various plants with a milky, poisonous sap that originated in America

molt: to shed skin in the process of growth

nectar: a sugary liquid made by plants to attract pollinating insects

Oyamel: a fir tree that serves as a roosting place for monarchs in the Mexican mountains

proboscis: a long tube that a monarch unrolls to suck nectar from flowers

pupa: a butterfly's resting stage in its chrysalis between larva and adult

thorax: the part of a butterfly's body between the head and the abdomen

transpiration: the release of water vapor from a leaf

Teacher Reflection

There is no need for teachers to know all the answers. One of the best things you can do for students is to serve as a model of a life-long learner. Use this reflection page to record some of your new understandings as you complete this unit.

What are some of your new understandings in regard to teaching and learning about this subject?

What in this unit worked for your students?

What were some problems that arose?

How could you overcome those problems next time?

What are some other things you would like to remind yourself about this study for next time?

References

Ballou, Mildred. 1986. "Taking the Icks and Yucks out of Science." *Science and Children* 23: 6–8.

Bruner, J. 1960. *The Process of Education.* Cambridge, Mass.: Harvard University Press.

Buzan, Tony. 1983. *Use Both Sides of Your Brain: New Techniques to Help You Read Efficiently, Study Effectively, Solve Problems, Remember More, Think Creatively.* Rev. ed. New York: Dutton.

Caine, Geoffrey, Renate Numella Caine, and Sam Crowell. 1999. *MindShifts: A Brain-Compatible Process for Professional Development and the Renewal of Education.* Tucson, Ariz.: Zephyr Press.

Carroll, Kathleen. 1999. *Sing a Song of Science.* Tucson, Ariz.: Zephyr Press.

Cohen, Robert. 1999. "The Development and Use of a Constructivist Taxonomy in Elementary Education Teacher Training." Ph.D. diss., University of Maryland.

Cornell, Joseph. 1989. *Sharing the Joy of Nature.* Nevada City, Calif.: Dawn Publications.

Curriculum and Evaluation Standards for School Mathematics. 1989. Reston, Va.: National Council of Teachers of Mathematics.

D'Arcangelo, Marcia. 1998. "The Brains behind the Brain." *Educational Leadership* 56, 3: 20–25.

Find it! Science: The Books You Need at Lightning Speed. CD-ROM. Armonk, N.Y.: The Learning Team.

Fosmet, Catherine Twomey. 1993. Preface in *In Search of Understanding: The Case for Construcivist Classrooms,* by Jacqueline Brooks and Martin Brooks. Alexandria, Va.: ASCD.

Gardner, Howard. 1983. *Frames of Mind.* New York: Basic.

Jensen, Eric. 1995. *Brain-Based Learning and Teaching.* Del Mar, Calif.: Turning Point.

———. 1994. *The Learning Brain.* Del Mar, Calif.: Turning Point.

———. 1998. *Teaching with the Brain in Mind.* Alexandria, Va.: ASCD.

Kellert, Stephen, ed. 1995. *The Biophilia Hypothesis.* Covelo, Calif.: Island Press.

Langer, Ellen. 1997. *The Power of Mindful Learning.* Reading, Mass.: Addison-Wesley.

Liem, Tik L. 1992. *Invitations to Science Inquiry.* Chino Hills, Calif.: Science Inquiry Enterprises.

Lowery, Lawrence. 1998. "How New Science Curriculums Reflect Brain Research." *Educational Leadership* 56, 3: 26–31.

———, ed. 1997. *NSTA Pathways to the Science Standards: Guidelines for Moving the Vision into Practice.* Arlington, Va.: National Science Teachers Association.

Lozanov, G. 1981. *Suggestology and Outlines of Suggstopedia.* New York: Gordon and Breach.

Lyman, Frank. 1998. "Critical and Creative Thinking: Tapping the Power of Your Mind." In Carol Carter, Joyce Bishop, and Sarah Lyman Kravitts, eds. *Keys to Success: How to Achieve Your Goals.* 2d ed. Upper Saddle River, N.J.: Prentice Hall.

———. 1992. "Think-Pair-Share, Think Trix, Thinklinks, and Weird Facts: Antri System for Cooperative Thinking." In Neil Davidson, ed. *Enhancing Thinking through Cooperation*. New York: Columbia Teachers College Press.

Margulies, Nancy. 1991. *Mapping Inner Space: Learning and Teaching Mind Mapping*. Tucson, Ariz.: Zephyr Press.

Martin, Lee. 1999. "Productive Questions: Tools for Supporting Constructivist Learning." *Science and Children* 23: 24–28.

National Science Education Standards. 1996. Washington, D.C.: National Academy Press.

Nebel, Bernard, and Richard Wright. 1993. *Environmental Science: The Way the World Works*. Englewood Cliffs, N.J.: Simon and Schuster.

Palmer, Parker. 1998. *The Courage to Teach*. San Francisco, Calif.: Jossey-Bass.

Resnick, Lauren B. 1987. *Education and Learning to Think*. Washington, D.C.: National Academy Press.

Saul, Wendy, and Jeanne Reardon, eds. 1996. *Beyond the Science Kit*. Portsmouth, N.H.: Heinemann.

Sprenger, Marilee. 1999. *Learning and Memory: The Brain in Action*. Arlington, Va.: ASCD.

Sylwester, Robert. 1998. "Art for the Brain's Sake." *Educational Leadership* 56, 3: 31–35.

A Teacher's Guide to Performance-Based Learning and Assessment by the Educators of Connecticut's Pompraug School District. 1996. Arlington, Va.: ASCD.

Urquhart, Fred A. 1987. *The Monarch Butterfly: International Traveler*. Chicago: Nelson-Hall.

Weinberger, Norman. 1998. "The Music of Our Minds." *Educational Leadership* 56, 3: 36–40.

Wiggins, Grant, and Jay McTighe. 1998. *Understanding by Design*. Alexandria. Va.: ASCD.

Singers, Actors, and Musicians on the CD

Joe Brady: voice, guitar, and music composer for "Scientific Method Blues" and "Plant Song"; chorus, solos

Benjamin Carroll: vocal for "Butterfly Song"

Jon Michael Carroll: harmonica on "Scientific Method Blues"

Kathleen Carroll: writer, producer, chorus for "Susie Sound Wave"; narrator for Monarch to Mexico

Steve Carroll: Giant's voice in "Metric Song"; artwork

Chialin Chang: chorus, solos

Gil Glass: chorus, Mr. Variable, Salvadore Sound Wave, Ben Franklin, Galvani, Michael Faraday, Thomas Edison, narrator

Ollie Harma: guitar for "Scientific Method Blues"

Michelle Jackson: chorus, solos, Valerie Variable, Michelle, Heather

Gwen Jenifer: musical director, synthesizer, chorus, solos, composer of "Adaptations," "Food Chain"

Shade Jenifer: music composer and rapper for "Vibrations" and "Electric Connections"; chorus, solo

Joseph Babarsky: Vinny Variable, Wilbert

Nick Kendall: violin in "Plant Song," "Food Chain," "Monarch to Mexico," percussion in "The Monarch Song"

Mary Khananayev: chorus, solos

Mi Sui Ling: chorus

Yan-fang Parsons: chorus, solos

Catherine Razi: wrote "Electric Connections Rap"

Hugh Scott: rapper for "Vibrations" and "Electric Connections," Thales, Volta

Betty Yelana Simkin: female vocal for "The Monarch Song"

Lisa Solomon: chorus

Angie Terry: chorus

Ruth Turner: chorus, solos

Note: A song about metric measurement is included on the CD to inspire you to build your own unit on measurement using the Science for Every Learner *format.*

Appendix

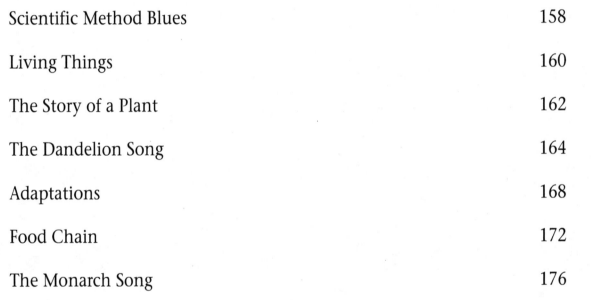

 *Musical Scores*

Scientific Method Blues

Words and Music by
Kathleen Carroll

Living Things

Words by Kathleen Carroll

Music by Gwen Jenifer

From the small - est cell to the tall - est tree,_____
an - i - mals and plants are a - live like me. We all need air, some
ox - y - gen to breathe, wa - ter and food and a place to be...
Hey! It's great to be a - live!_____ The world is our home it's a home to share.
Hey! It's great to be a - live!_____ Let's show the earth we care!

Ev' - ry liv - ing thing can grow and
Each of us must have the heart to

re - pro - duce it - self you know. And death is some - thing liv - ing
care e - nough to do our part. And look for ways to

things must face so new gen - er - a - tions can
save not waste so we all can live in a

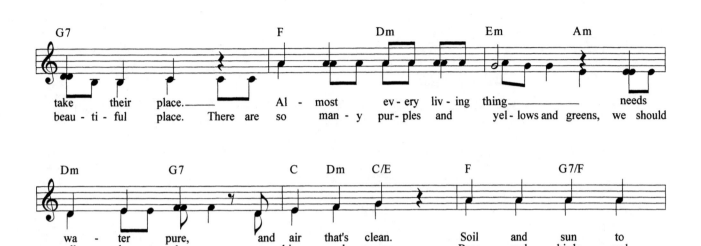

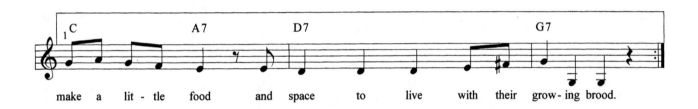

The Story of a Plant

Words by Kathleen Carroll

Music by Joe Brady

The Dandelion Song

Words and music by
Kathleen Carroll

166   *The Dandelion Song*

Adaptations

Words by Kathleen Carroll

Music by Gwen Jenifer

Food Chain

Words by Kathleen Carroll

Music by Gwen Jenifer

Refrain

'Round and 'round the en-er-gy goes; 'round and 'round in the food chain._____ The

sun is the source of the en - er - gy that goes a - round in the food chain.

Verse 1.

The sun is the source of the en - er - gy in you and me and ev-'ry thing we see. And

green plants store sun's en - er - gy as food so liv - ing things can be._____ The

(Spoken) *The energy goes...*

from the sun to the plants to the herb - i - vores_____ who pass the

en - er - gy to the car - ni - vores._____ So the

car - ni - vores die and their bo - dies de - cay._____ They give their

To Refrain

en - er - gy back to the plants that way._____ Oh...

174   *Food Chain*

The Monarch Song

Words and music by
Kathleen Carroll

The *Scientific Method Blues* Dance

Below you will find the words to the *Scientific Method Blues* with the accompanying directions for the dance. Try it out!

1. *If you have a question*
   (Cup one elbow with one hand. Extend the other arm vertically with your hand curved like a question mark.)

2. *You want to test*
   (Hold up an imaginary test tube in one hand. Wave the other hand in front of it with your finger pointing.)

3. *You've got to make your...Hypothesis.*
   (With your elbow bent, point to your head with your index finger then extend the same arm out straight.)

4. *For your guess to be smart*
   (With both elbows bent, point to your head with both index fingers.)

5. *Gotta do your part.*
   (Cross your arms over your chest, making an X shape.)

6. *Get the research before you start.*
   (Make a rolling motion with your hands as if you are gathering something toward you.)

7. *Oh, the Scientific Method, it's the way to go, yes it is.*
    Yes, the Scientific Method, if you want to...
   (Wave your hands above your head from side to side in time to the music.)

8. *Show...*
   (With one knee bent, extend the other leg and opposite arm, as in, "It's show time!")

Science for Every Learner, © 2000 Zephyr Press, Tucson, Arizona

9. *What you know.*
    (With both elbows bent, point to your head with both index fingers.)

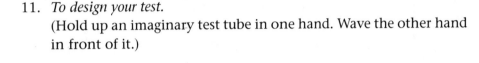

10. *And now you're set*
    (Bend your elbows. Place your hands, fingers pointing to the front, with the palms facing each other directly in front of you.)

11. *To design your test.*
    (Hold up an imaginary test tube in one hand. Wave the other hand in front of it.)

12. *Change one variable.*
    (Bend your elbows. Place your hands, palms facing each other, in front of you and to your left.)

13. *Control the rest.*
    (Bend your elbows. Place your hands, palms facing each other, in front of you and to your right.)

14. *Then you get your data.*
    (Make a rolling motion with your hands as if you are gathering something toward you.)

15. *That's numbers to you.*
    (Hold your hands above your head and wiggle your fingers.)

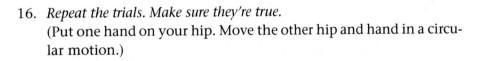

16. *Repeat the trials. Make sure they're true.*
    (Put one hand on your hip. Move the other hip and hand in a circular motion.)

17. *Oh, the Scientific Method, it's the way to go, yes it is.*
    Yes, the Scientific Method, if you want to...
    (Wave your hands above your head from side to side in time to the music.)

Science for Every Learner, © 2000 Zephyr Press, Tucson, Arizona

18. *Show...*
    (With one knee bent, extend the other leg and opposite arm, as in, "It's show time!")

19. *What you know.*
    (With both elbows bent, point to your head with both index fingers.)

20. *Keep a record. Keep it in a book.*
    (Bring your hands together with the palms open and your little fingers touching to look like a book.)

21. *If anyone asks you, say, "Take a look!"*
    (Hold up the palm of one hand and point to it with your other hand.)

22. *And make a graph...*
    (Bend your left elbow with your left forearm pointing straight up to look like the y-axis of a graph. Extend your right arm to represent the x-axis of a graph.)

23. *The results to cite.*
    (Keeping your left arm in place as the y-axis, draw an imaginary line on your imaginary graph with your right hand.)

24. *Then draw the conclusions.*
    (Make a rolling motion with your hands as if you are gathering something toward you.)

25. *Were you wrong or right?*
    (With your elbows by your sides and the palms up, raise one palm and then the other in a shrugging motion.)

26. *Oh, it really doesn't matter.*
    (Place one hand on your hip. Shake your head from side to side and shake your index finger in front of you.)

27. *You just want to know.*
    (With both elbows bent, point to your head with both index fingers.)

28. *Right or wrong is not the question.*
    (With your elbows by your sides and the palms up, raise one palm and then the other, in a shrugging motion)

29. *You just want to show…*
    (With one knee bent, extend the other leg and opposite arm, as in, "It's show time!")

30. *What you know.*
    (With both elbows bent, point to your head with both index fingers.)

31. *Ooh, yeah! That's right.*
    (Extend your arms above your head with attitude!)

182

The Metric Song

This song can be heard on the accompanying CD.

Refrain:
Oh, metric you're the one.
You make measuring more fun.
Based on ten. Let's start again
And go the metric way.

There once was a family of giants
And Kilo was their name.
They were all so huge and tall
And no two were the same.

Now, Kilogram, he weighed a lot
And Kilometer was long.
Kiloliter was big and wet.
Each one was a thousand strong.

Refrain

There also were some tiny elves
Who had the name of Milli.
One one thousandth—they're so small
To think of them seems silly!

Refrain

Now milligrams, they don't weigh much.
And millimeters are short.
A milliliter's a tiny drop
Of liquid they report.

Refrain

So, grams you may have noticed
Are things you can weigh.
Length is meter, liquid's liter.
That's the metric way.

Refrain

Science for Every Learner, © 2000 Zephyr Press, Tucson, Arizona

About the Author

Kathleen Carroll, M.Ed., is a senior faculty member and college supervisor for a master's degree completion program at Cambridge College. She teaches Using the Multiple Intelligences in the Classroom and Teaching for Scientific Understanding to master's degree candidates. She is an author and instructor for a regional training center, where she is involved in designing a master's course in assessment techniques. Her workshops and other presentations feature such topics as classroom assessment, science education, classroom applications of the multiple intelligences, and brain-compatible teaching techniques. Kathleen received her bachelor of arts degree from Catholic University and her master of education degree in accelerated learning from Cambridge College.

Add Stories, Raps, and Songs to Make Science Fun to Learn

SING A SONG OF SCIENCE

Kathleen Carroll, M.Ed.

featuring Gwendolyn Jenifer and the students of the Duke Ellington School of the Arts

Here's a brain-friendly approach to science and a new way to teach it! You'll find that songs, raps, and stories are indispensable tools to reinforce science concepts your children are learning. Get started with an easy-to-read overview of brain-friendly teaching that touches on the work of Howard Gardner, Marian Diamond, and Robert Sylwester.

Combine this innovative approach to reinforce fundamental science facts. *Sing a Song of Science* covers 16 topics, including—

- Matter and energy

Each topic includes tw... ...truct their own understanding with the hands-on kinesth... ...heir learning with activities to reinforce the vocabulary a... ...u and your children will be able to keep up-to-date with a...

Grades K–6
35-minute CD and 64-pa...
ISBN: 1-56976-090-X
1094-W . . . $27.00

Order Form

Qty.	Item #	
	1094-W	Sin...

Name _____
Address _____
City _____
State _____
Phone (_____) _____
E-mail _____

Method of payment (check one):

☐ Check or Money Order   ☐ Visa
☐ MasterCard   ☐ Purchase Order Attached
Credit Card No. _____
Expires _____
Signature _____

Total (U.S. funds only)

CANADA: add 30% for S & H and G.S.T.

☎ Please include your phone number in case we have questions about your order.

Call, Write, Fax, or e-mail for your FREE Catalog!

Zephyr Press

P.O. Box 66006-W
Tucson, AZ 85728-6006

1-800-232-2187
520-322-5090
FAX 520-323-9402
neways2learn@zephyrpress.com

Order these resources and more any time, day or night, online at www.zephyrpress.com or www.i-home-school.com